TAKE ME TO FRANCE

*A French Phrase Book for the
American Soldier*

By

CLAUDE MICHELON

On Temporary Furlough from
the French Army

UNIFORM
PRESS

Uniform Press Ltd
66 Charlotte Street
London
W1T 4QE

www.uniformpress.com

10 9 8 7 6 5 4 3 2 1

This edition published in 2015
First published in 1917 by the Bobbs-Merrill Company

ISBN 978-1-910500-03-3

Printed in India by Imprint Digital.

TAKE ME TO FRANCE

*A French Phrase Book for the
American Soldier*

By

CLAUDE MICHELON

On Temporary Furlough from
the French Army

UNIFORM
PRESS

PREFACE

The author, having witnessed the difficulties encountered by the French Army at the beginning of the war for lack of understanding the English language, is prompted to give the American soldiers the results of his experiences by means of this booklet. It comprises the necessary elements of the daily field conversation of the Franco-American Armies as well as guidance for those traveling in France.

Twenty years of teaching have enabled the author to condense into a booklet of this size such grammatical rules as are indispensable, and all the words and sentences necessary to fulfil its purpose. It is, then, a simple, brief guide which will be of great benefit to all, beginners as well as those having some knowledge of the language, who intend to visit France.   C. M.

CONTENTS

TAKE ME TO FRANCE

TAKE ME TO FRANCE

I

Simple Essentials of Language and Grammar

PRONUNCIATION

FRENCH ALPHABET

French	Pronunciation
A	*Ah*
B	*Bay*
C	*Say*
D	*Day*
E	*Eh* (short)
F	*Eff*
G	*Zheh*
H	*Ash*
I	*Ee*
J	*Zhee*
K	*Kah*
L	*Ell*
M	*Emm*
N	*Enn*
O	*Oh*
P	*Pay*
Q	*Ku*
R	*Err*
S	*Ess*
T	*Tay*
U	This letter cannot be imitated. Try *ewu*

V	*Vay*
X	*Eeks*
Y	*Ee–greck*
Z	*Zed*

VOWELS

a	as in *papa*
â	as in *father*
e	as in *the*
é	as in *café*
è	like *e* in *let*
ê	like the *a* in *care*
i	like *ee* in *Lee*
y	like *ee* in *Lee*
o	as in *pope*
ô	as in *ohl* but longer
u	has no equivalent in English. Try *ewu* or ask a native
ai and ei	as in *air*
au	as in *beau*
ay	as in *pay*
eu and oe	like the *u* in *fur*
ou	like *oo* in *Coo-coo*
oi	like *oh* or *wah*. Ex.—Moi (me) like *mwah*

NASAL SOUNDS

An, ant, en, ent in adverbs, like *ahng*
On, like *ong*. Ex.—Bon (good) like *bong*
Un (m) like *ughn*, or, if you prefer, just grunt
Une (f) like *uhne*

The ending "tion" is pronounced *seeong*, and the meaning is the same in both languages.

"Able" at the end of adjectives is pronounced *ahble*. *Ah* (long) and *ble* (short).

"Ant," present participle ending, corresponds to the English "ing" and is always pronounced *ahng*.

ACCENTS

There are three accents in French, which really constitute the musical part of the language.

The *accent aigu* (acute) indicated by the mark ´ which tends to raise or sharp the accent.

The *accent grave* (grave) indicated by the mark ` which tends to lower or flat the accent.

The *accent circonflexe* (circumflex)indicated by the mark ^ which tends to hold the accent.

LIAISON

The linking or (liaison) of two words in French is the pronouncing of the last consonant of a word with the first syllable of the next word when it begins with a vowel or mute "h."

Venez ici (*vaynay zeecee*) come here

The letter "e" without an accent is called mute and is never pronounced.

Note: The above pronunciation is just a skeleton key of the French language. Many other rules should be given but the lack of space forbids. The best way is to ask a native when opportunity presents itself.

GENDER

There are only two genders in the French language, masculine and feminine. Only a thorough knowledge of French will enable you to distinguish the gender of inanimate things.

As a rule all words ending in "e" are feminine.

There is no neuter gender.

ARTICLES

The Definite Article

The definite article *the* is rendered in French by *le* before a masculine noun; by *la* before a feminine noun; and by *les* before the plural of both genders.

> Le (m. sing.)
> La (f. sing.)
> Les (m. and f. pl.)

Before a vowel or a silent "h" suppress "e" or "a" and replace it by an apostrophe (').

> L'enfant The child
> L'eau The water
> L'homme The man

> "Of the," "From the"

> Du (m. sing.)
> De la (f. sing.)
> Des (m. and f. pl.)

Never say "de le" or "de les." While "de" means "of" or "from" it should never be combined with the article "the" to say "of the" or "from the."

Instead use the correct forms as given above.

> "To the" or "At the"

> Au (m. sing.)
> A la (f. sing.)
> Aux (m. and f. pl.)

Never say "à le" for "to the" or "at the." While "à" is the preposition "to" it should never be combined with the article "the" to say "to the."

Instead use the correct forms as given above.

> "Of them," "From them," "Some"
> Des (m. and f. pl.)

THE INDEFINITE ARTICLE

A, An, or Some

Un (m. sing.)	Like *un* in *hunter*
Une (f. sing.)	*uhne*
Des (m. and f. pl.)	*day*
Un soldat (a soldier)	*Un soldah*
Une batterie (a battery)	*Uhne battree*
Des munitions (some munitions)	*Day muneeseeong*

ADJECTIVES

The French adjectives usually follow the noun and agree in gender and number.

Les tranchées sont larges et profondes.

The trenches are wide and deep.

Exceptions will not be mentioned for brevity's sake.

DEMONSTRATIVE

This or That

Ce (m. sing.)	Pronounced *seh*, is used before consonants
Cet (m. sing.)	Pronounced *set*, is used before vowels or silent "h"
Cette (f. sing.)	Pronounced *set*
Ces (m. and f. pl.)	Pronounced *say*. Means "these" or "those"

POSSESSIVE

The possessive adjectives agree with the object possessed and not with the possessor. Observe this rule carefully as it is just the reverse of the English language.

Singular		Plural		
MASCULINE	FEMININE	MASCULINE AND FEMININE		
Mon (*mong*)	Ma (*mah*)	Mes (*may*)	My	
Ton (*tong*)	Ta (*tah*)	Tes (*tay*)	Thy	
Son (*song*)	Sa (*sah*)	Ses (*say*)	His, her, its	
Notre (*nohtr*)	Notre	Nos (*noh*)	Our	
Votre (*vohtr*)	Votre	Vos (*voh*)	Your	
Leur (*eu* like *ur* in *fur*)	Leur	Leurs	Their	

PRONOUNS

PERSONAL

Singular		Plural	
Je (*jeh*)	I	Nous (*noo*)	We
Tu (*tuh*)	Thou	Vous (*voo*)	You
Il (*eel*)	He	Ils (*eel*)	They (m.)
Elle (*el*)	She	Elles (*el*)	They (f.)

RELATIVE

Qui (*kee*)	Who, which, that
Quoi (*kouah*)	What, that
Quel (*kel*)	
Lequel (*lehkel*)	Which
Que (*keh*)	That, which

THE FRENCH VERB

The greatest difficulty the student will encounter in the French language is the understanding and the application of the verb. It would be nonsense to try to teach the French verb thoroughly in a few lessons, but by using the following rules more results can be accomplished than by years of study in a mechanical way.

The first thing to know is the mechanism of the two auxiliary verbs "to have" and "to be."

AUXILIARY VERB

"To have"

Avoir (*ahvoahr*)	To have
Ayant (*ayeeahn*)	Having
Eu (*ew*)	Had

PRESENT

J'ai (*jay*)	I have
Tu as (*tuh ah*)	Thou hast
Il a (*eel ah*)	He has
Elle a (*el ah*)	She has
Nous avons (*noo-za-vong*)	We have
Vous avez (*voo-za-vay*)	You have
Ils ont (m.) (*eel-zong*)	They have
Elles ont (f.) (*el zong*)	They have

FUTURE

J'aurai (*j'oray*)	I shall or will have
Tu auras (*tuh orah*)	Thou shalt or wilt have
Il aura (*eel orah*)	He shall or will have
Elle aura (*el orah*)	She shall or will have
Nous aurons (*noo-zo-rong*)	We shall or will have
Vous aurez (*voo-zo-ray*)	You shall or will have
Ils auront (*eel-zo-rong*)	They shall or will have
Elles auront (*el-zo-rong*)	They shall or will have

THE PAST INDEFINITE OR PERFECT

This tense is used to express past time in daily conversation.

J'ai eu (*j'ay eu*)	I have had
Tu as eu (*tuh ah eu*)	Thou hast had
Il a eu (*eel ah eu*)	He has had
Elle a eu (*el ah eu*)	She has had
Nous avons eu (*noo-za-von-zeu*)	We have had
Vous avez eu (*voo-za-vay-zeu*)	You have had

Ils ont eu (*eel–zon–teu*)   They have had
Elles ont eu (*el–zon–teu*)   They have had

"To be"

Etre (*aytr*)   To be
Etant (*attang*)   Being
Eté (*ay–tay*)   Been

PRESENT

Je suis (*jeh swee*)   I am
Tu es (*tuh ay ay–tay*)   Thou art
Il est (*eel ay*)   He is
Elle est (*el ay*)   She is
Nous sommes (*noo somm*)   We are
Vous êtes (*voo–zait*)   You are
Ils sont (*eel song*)   They are
Elles sont (*el song*)   They are

FUTURE

Je serai été (*jeh serray*)   I shall or will be
Tu seras (*tuh serrah*)   Thou shalt or wilt be
Il sera (*eel serrah*)   He shall or will be
Elle sera (*el serrah*)   She shall or will be
Nous serons (*noo serrong*)   We shall or will be
Vous serez (*voo serray*)   You shall or will be
Ils seront (*eel serrong*)   They shall or will be
Elles seront (*el serrong*)   They shall or will be

THE PAST INDEFINITE OR PERFECT

J'ai été (*jay ay–tay*)   I have been
Tu as été (*tuh ah ay-tay*)   Thou hast been
Il a été (*eel ah ay–tay*)   He has been
Elle a été (*el ah ay-tay*)   She has been
Nous avons été (*noo–za–vong–zay–tay*)   We have been

Vous avez été (*voo-za-vay-zay-tay*)		You have been
Ils ont été (*eel-zon-tay-tay*)		They have been
Elles ont été (*el-zon-tay-tay*)		They have been

Always remember and use the present tense of either the auxiliary verbs "to be" or "to have" with the past participle of all French verbs, without exception, to express the Conversational Past.

All verbs expressing a violent motion, and some others, take the present tense of "to be" instead of "to have," as:

Aller (*allay*)	To go
Venir (*vayneer*)	To come
Sortir (*sorteer*)	To go out
Entrer (*angtray*)	To enter
Monter (*mongtay*)	To mount
Descendre (*daysendruh*)	To descend
Tomber (*tombay*)	To fall

As a *general rule* to express the past for conversation take the present tense of "to have" with the past participle of the verb you desire to use and usually you will be right, and should you make a mistake they will smile at you and correct the error.

A verb that stands alone and that ends in "ez" (pronounced like the English "a") *generally* expresses a *command*.

Ecrivez	Write	Apprenez	Learn
Lisez	Read	Suprenez	Surprise
Parlez	Speak	Répétez	Repeat
Ecoutez	Listen	Fermez	Close
Venez	Come	Ouvrez	Open
Marchez	March	Allez	Go
Montez	Mount	Mettez	Place
Descendez	Descend	Surmettez	Place above
Effacez	Erase	Démettez	Put out, dismiss
Prenez	Take	Permettez	Permit
Comprenez	Comprehend	Admettez	Admit

The prefix "re" placed before a verb means "again."

Reprenez	Take again
Remettez	Place again
Remarchez	March again
Revenez	Come again

THE POSITION OF THE PRONOUN IN RELATION TO THE VERB

(1) Placing the pronoun "vous" ("you" pronounced as *voo*) before the verb indicates that the verb is in declarative.

Vous écrivez	You write, you are writing, you do write
Vous parlez	You speak, you are speaking, you do speak
Vous marchez	You march, you are marching, you do march
Vous prenez	You take, you are taking, you do take
Vous apprenez	You learn, you are learning, you do learn

Note that the three forms in English are condensed into one in French.

(2) Placing the pronoun after the verb indicates that it is a question.

Parlez–vous?	Do you speak?
Ecrivez–vous?	Do you write?
Admettez–vous?	Do you admit?
Apprenez–vouz?	Do you learn?
Comprenez–vous?	Do you comprehend?

Note that when the pronoun is placed after the verb it is connected to the verb by a dash or hyphen.

THE ENDING "ONS"

The sound "ons" (pronounced *ong*) at the end of a verb means "let us" and indicates that the verb is in the imperative mode.

Ecrivons	Let us write
Lisons	Let us read
Parlons	Let us speak
Comprenons	Let us comprehend

Placing "nous" (meaning "we") before a verb standing alone ending in "ons" indicates that the action is going on or that the verb is in the present tense.

> Nous écrivons   We write, we are writing, we do write
> Nous lisons   We read, we are reading, we do read

Note that all three forms in English are reduced to one in French.

THE ENDING OF THE VERB IN THE THIRD PERSON PLURAL

The verb in the third person plural always ends in "nt" but the ending is never pronounced. It is merely a grammatical rule to indicate the third person plural.

> Ils viennent   They come

THE FUTURE OF ALL FRENCH VERBS

To learn the future of all French verbs, without exception, whether regular, irregular, or reflexive, learn and use the following endings:

	With	Root of Verb	Put	
Singular	je		rai	(will or shall)
	tu		ras	(will or shall)
	il		ra	(will or shall)
	elle		ra	(will or shall)
	on (one)		ra	(will or shall)
Plural	nous		rons	(will or shall)
	vous		rez	(will or shall)
	ils		ront	(will or shall)
	elles		ront	(will or shall)

For each pronoun use its corresponding ending added to the root of the verb. If you don't know, guess it, and some one will correct you. In conversation the difference between "will" and "shall" is indicated by the determination of your gesture.

The Conditional

With each pronoun use its corresponding ending added to the root of the verb in the same way as you formed the Future Tense. Here again the difference between "would or should" in conversation must be indicated by your gesture.

Singular	With	Root of Verb	Put	
	je		rais	(would or should)
	tu		rais	(would or should)
	il		rait	(would or should)
	elle		rait	(would or should)
	on		rait	(would or should)
Plural	nous		rions	(would or should)
	vous		riez	(would or should)
	ils		riez	(would or should)
	elles		raient	(would or should)

Conjugations

There are four conjugations in the French language and they are recognized by the following endings of the present infinitive:

First Conjugation, "er," as in aimer, to love.
Second Conjugation, "ir," as in finir, to finish.
Third Conjugation, "oir," as in recevoir, to receive.
Fourth Conjugation, "re," as in vendre, to sell.

Present Participle

The Present Participle always ends in "ant" and means the same as the English "ing."

Aimant	Loving
Finissant	Finishing
Recevant	Receiving
Vendant	Selling

The Past Participle

The Past Participle can only end in one of three ways:

In the first conjugation, "é," as in aimé, loved.

In the second conjugation, "i," as in fini, finished.

In the third and fourth conjugation, "u," as in reçu, received, and vendu, sold.

Forms of Verbs

There are *regular, irregular, impersonal,* and *reflexive verbs.*

The *regular* verbs are those which the root never changes.

The *irregular* verbs are those in which the root changes.

The *impersonal* verbs are those which are only conjugated in the third person of the singular, as:

> Il pleut (*eel plew*)   It rains
> Il neige (*eel naig*)   It snows

The *reflexive* verbs are those which reflect the action on the subject.

The Three Necessary Tenses

As this is not a grammar we will only give the three most important tenses that the student should know: the present, the future, and the past indefinite.

These three are all that a student needs to carry on and understand a daily conversation.

The following are examples of each of the four conjugations in the three most important tenses, the present, the future and the conversational past—the verbs in each case being *regular.*

Model of the First Regular Conjugation, "Er"

Conjugation of the verb Parler, to speak

> Parler   To speak
> Parlant   Speaking
> Parlé   Spoke

I speak, I am speaking, I do speak, etc.

je	parl–e (*jeh pahrl*)
tu	parl–es (*tuh pahrl*)
il	parl–e (*eel pahrl*)
elle	parl–e (*el pahrl*)
on	parl–e (*on pahrl*)
nous	parl–ons (*noo pahrl ong*)
vous	parl–ez (*voo pahrl ay*)
ils	parl–ent (*eel pahrl*) ("nt" never pronounced)
elles	parl–ent (*el pahrl*) ("nt" never pronounced)

FUTURE

I shall or will speak, etc.

je	parle–rai (*jeh pahrl ray*)
tu	parle–ras (*tuh pahrl rah*)
il	parle–ra (*eel pahrl rah*)
elle	parle–ra (*el pahrl rah*)
on	parle–ra (*on pahrl rah*)
nous	parle–rons (*noo pahrl rong*)
vous	parle–rez (*voo pahrl ray*)
ils	parle–ront (*eel pahrl rong*)
elles	parle–ront (*el pahrl rong*)

CONVERSATIONAL PAST

Rule: Use the present tense of the auxiliary verb "to have" with the past participle of the verb you desire to use.

I spoke, I have spoken, I did speak, etc.

j'ai	parlé
tu as	parlé
il a	parlé
elle a	parlé

on a	parlé
nous avons	parlé
vous avez	parlé
ils ont	parlé
elles ont	parlé

MODEL OF THE SECOND REGULAR CONJUGATION, "IR"

Conjugation of the verb Finir, to finish

Finir (*feeneer*)	To finish
Finissant (*feeneessahng*)	Finishing
Fini (*feenee*)	Finished

PRESENT

I finish, I am finishing, I do finish, etc.

je	fini–s (*jeh feenee*)
tu	fini–s (*tuh feenee*)
il	fini–t (*eel feenee*)
elle	fini–t (*el feenee*)
nous	fini–ssons (*noo feeneessong*)
vous	fini–ssez (*voo feeneessay*)
ils	fini–ssent (*eel feeneess*)
elles	fini–ssent (*el feeneess*)

FUTURE

I shall or will finish, etc.

je	fini–rai (*jeh feeneeray*)
tu	fini–ras (*tuh feeneerah*)
il	fini–ra (*eel feeneerah*)
elle	fini–ra (*el feeneerah*)
nous	fini–rons (*noo feeneerong*)
vous	fini–rez (*voo feeneeray*)
ils	fini–ront (*eel feeneerong*)
elles	fini–ront (*el feeneerong*)

CONVERSATIONAL PAST

I finished, I have finished, I did finish, etc.

j'ai	fini
tu as	fini
il a	fini
elle a	fini
nous avons	fini
vous avez	fini
ils ont	fini
elles ont	fini

MODEL OF THE THIRD REGULAR CONJUGATION, "OIR"

Conjugation of the verb Recevoir, to receive

Recevoir (*ressevoahr*)	To receive
Recevant (*ressevahng*)	Receiving
Reçu (*ressuh*)	Received

PRESENT

I receive, I am receiving, I do receive, etc.

je	reçoi–s (*jeh ressouah*)
tu	reçoi–s (*tuh ressouah*)
il	reçoi–t (*eel ressouah*)
elle	reçoi–t (*el ressouah*)
nous	recev–ons (*noo ressvong*)
vous	recev–ez (*voo ressvay*)
ils	reçoiv–ent (*eel ressouahv*)
elles	reçoiv–ent (*el ressouahv*)

FUTURE

I shall or will receive, etc.

je	recev–rai (*jeh ressvray*)
tu	recev–ras (*tuh ressvrah*)
il	recev–ra (*eel ressvrah*)

elle	recev–ra (*el ressvrong*)
nous	recev–rons (*noo ressvrong*)
vous	recev–rez (*voo ressvray*)
ils	recev–ront (*eel ressvrong*)
elles	recev–ront (*el ressvrong*)

CONVERSATIONAL PAST

I received, I have received, I did receive, etc.

j'ai	reçu
tu as	reçu
il a	reçu
elle a	reçu
nous avons	reçu
vous avez	reçu
ils ont	reçu
elles ont	reçu

MODEL OF THE FOURTH REGULAR CONJUGATION, "RE"

Conjugation of the verb Vendre, to sell

Vendre (*vahndr*)	To sell
Vendant (*vahndang*)	Selling
Vendu (*vahndue*)	Sold

PRESENT

I sell, I am selling, I do sell, etc.

je	vend–s (*jeh vahng*)
tu	vend–s (*tu vahng*)
il	vend (*eel vahng*)
elle	vend (*el vahng*)
nous	vend–ons (*noo vahngdong*)
vous	vend–ez (*voo vahngday*)
ils	vend–ent (*eel vahngd*)
elles	vend–ent (*el vahngd*)

FUTURE

I shall or will sell, etc.

je	vend–rai	(*jeh vahngdray*)
tu	vend–ras	(*tu vahngdrah*)
il	vend–ra	(*eel vahngdrah*)
elle	vend–ra	(*el vahngdrah*)
nous	vend–rons	(*noo vahngdrong*)
vous	vend–rez	(*voo vahndray*)
ils	vend–ront	(*eel vahngdrong*)
elles	vend–ront	(*el vahngdrong*)

CONVERSATIONAL PAST

I sold, I have sold, I did sell, etc.

j'ai	vendu
tu as	vendu
il a	vendu
elle a	vendu
nous avons	vendu
vous avez	vendu
ils ont	vendu
elles ont	vendu

We again call your attention to the *imperative mood*. When you want to *command* take "we" away from the present tense and what remains means "Let us."

Nous parlons   We speak   Parlons   Let us speak

In like manner if you take "you" away from the same tense that which remains means a direct command.

Vous parlez   You speak   Parlez   Speak

This is all that can be given about verbs in a short course. Should you need more, consult classical text books.

ADJECTIVES

In a work of this sort it has seemed wise to have the lists of words arranged in some manner likely to excite the soldier's attention and stimulate his memory. It is therefore with the hope of affording the memory the greatest possible assistance that in this and following lists a system of grouping words according to associated ideas has been used.

ENGLISH	FRENCH	PRONUNCIATION
absent	absent	*absahng*
present	présent	*prayzahng*
active	actif	*akteef*
lazy	paresseux	*pahrayseuh*
attentive	attentif	*ahtahngteef*
distracted	distrait	*deestray*
big	gros	*groh*
little	petit	*ptee*
large	grand	*grahng*
small	petit	*ptee*
brave	brave	*brahv*
cowardly	poltron	*poltrong*
free	libre	*leebr*
captive	captif	*kahpteef*
certain	certain	*sairtaing*
doubtful	douteux	*dooteuh*
clever	habile	*ahbeel*
stupid	stupide	*stupeed*
civil	civil	*seeveel*
military	militaire	*meeleetair*
courageous	courageux	*koorahjeuh*
timid	timide	*temeed*
light	clair	*clare*
dark	sombre	*sohmbr*

ENGLISH	FRENCH	PRONUNCIATION
deep	profond	*prohfong*
shallow	peu profond	*peu prohfong*
agreeable	agréable	*ah–gray–ahble*
disagreeable	désagréable	*day–zah–gray–ahble*
clean	propre	*propr*
dirty	sale	*sahl*
true	vrai	*vray*
false	faux	*foh*
famous	fameux	*fahmeuh*
unknown	inconnu	*an–kon–u*
fresh	frais	*fray*
stale	dur	*duhr*
frightful	affreux	*ah–freuh*
gay	gai	*gay*
good	bon	*bong*
bad	mauvais	*moh–vay*
high	haut	*oh*
low	bas	*bah*
hard	dur	*duhr*
soft	mou	*moo*
right	droit	*droah*
left	gauche	*gaush*
right	raison	*raysong*
wrong	tort	*toar*
heavy	lourd	*loor*
light	léger	*lay–jay*
long	long	*long*
short	court	*koor*
narrow	étroit	*ay–tro–ah*
wide	large	*lahrjeh*
open	ouvert	*oovayr*
closed	fermé	*fairmay*

ENGLISH	FRENCH	PRONUNCIATION
poor	pauvre	*pohvr*
rich	riche	*reesh*
pretty	joli	*johlee*
homely	laid	*lay*
ripe	mûr	*muhr*
rotten	pourri	*poor—ree*
happy	heureux	*no equivalent*
unhappy	malheureux	*no equivalent*
cheerful	joyeux	*joah—ee—euh*
sad	triste	*trist*
strong	fort	*fohr*
weak	faible	*faibl*
sweet	doux	*doo*
sour	aigre	*aygr*
lean	maigre	*maygr*
fat	gras	*grah*
round	rond	*rohng*
square	carré	*carray*
useful	utile	*uteel*
useless	inutile	*ee—nuteel*
warm	chaud	*show*
cold	froid	*froah*
dry	sec	*sehk*
wet	mouillé	*moo—ee—ay*
early	tôt	*toh*
late	tard	*tahr*
red	rouge	*rouge*
yellow	jaune	*johne*
black	noir	*noahr*
blue	bleu	*bleuh*
brown	brun	*brung*
gray	gris	*gree*

ENGLISH	FRENCH	PRONUNCIATION
green	vert	*vair*
violet	violet	*vee-o-lay*
white	blanc	*blahng*

The letter "u" and the sound *eu* in French have no imitation although the attempt has been made. Ask a native about them.

NUMERAL ADJECTIVES

ENGLISH	FRENCH	PRONUNCIATION
one	un	*ung*
two	deux	*deuh*
three	trois	*trouah*
four	quatre	*kahtr*
five	cinq	*sahnk*
six	six	*seece*
seven	sept	*set*
eight	huit	*wheet*
nine	neuf	*neuf*
ten	dix	*deece*
eleven	onze	*ongz*
twelve	douze	*dooze*
thirteen	treize	*trayz*
fourteen	quatorze	*katorz*
fifteen	quinze	*kangz*
sixteen	seize	*says*
seventeen	dix-sept	*deece set*
eighteen	dix-huit	*deez wheet*
nineteen	dix-neuf	*deez neuf*
twenty	vingt	*vengh*
twenty-one	vingt et un	*venghta ung*
twenty-two	vingt deux	*vengh deuh*
thirty	trente	*traunt*
thirty-one	trente et un	*traunta ung*
forty	quarante	*karaunt*

ENGLISH	FRENCH	PRONUNCIATION
forty-one	quarante et un	*karaunta ung*
fifty	cinquante	*sahnkaunt*
fifty-one	cinquante et un	*sahnkaunta ung*
fifty-two	cinquante-deux	*sahnkaunt deuh*
sixty	soixante	*soassaunt*
sixty-one	soixante et un	*soassaunta ung*
sixty-two	soixante-deux	*soassaunt deuh*
seventy	soixante-dix	*soassaunt deece*
seventy-one	soixante et onze	*soassaunta ongz*
seventy-two	soixante-douze	*soassaunt dooze*
eighty	quatre vingts	*katr vahng*
eighty-one	quatre-vingt-un	*katr vahng ung*
eighty-two	quatre-vingt-deux	*katr vahng deuh*
ninety	quatre-vingt-dix	*katr vahng deece*
ninety-one	quatre-vingt-onze	*katr vahng ongz*
ninety-two	quatre-vingt-douze	*katr vahng dooze*
one hundred	cent	*saung*
one hundred one	cent un	*saung ung*
one hundred two	cent deux	*saung deuh*
one hundred ten	cent dix	*saung deece*
one hundred eleven	cent onze	*saung ongz*
one hundred twelve	cent douze	*saung dooze*
one hundred twenty	cent vingt	*saung vahng*
one hundred twenty-one	cent vingt et un	*saung vahngt a ung*
one hundred thirty	cent trente	*saung traunt*
one hundred forty	cent quarante	*saung karaunt*
two hundred	deux cents	*deuh saung*
two hundred ten	deux cent dix	*deuh saung deece*
three hundred	trois cents	*trouah saung*
one thousand	mille	*meel*
two thousand	deux mille	*deuh meel*
ten thousand	dix mille	*dee meel*
one hundred thousand	cent mille	*saung meel*
one million	un million	*ung meelyong*

VERBS

English	French	Pronunciation	Past Participle of Irregular Verbs
to eat	manger	*maunjay*	
to drink	boire	*bouahr*	bu
to breakfast	déjeuner	*dayjeunay*	
to dine	dîner	*deenay*	
to sup	souper	*soopay*	
to be thirsty	avoir soif	*avouahr souaf*	
to be hungry	avoir faim	*avouahr fang*	
to be cold	avoir froid	*avouahr frouah*	
to be warm	avoir chaud	*avouahr show*	
to be in need of	avoir besoin	*avouahr beuhzouang*	
to serve	servir	*sehrveer*	servi
to carve	trancher	*traunshay*	
to cut	couper	*coopay*	
to sneeze	éternuer	*aytairnuay*	
to cough	tousser	*toossay*	
to think	penser	*paungsay*	
to reflect	réfléchir	*rayflaysheer*	
to speak	parler	*parlay*	
to say	dire	*deer*	dit
to repeat	répéter	*raypaytay*	
to explain	déclarer	*dayclarray*	
to ask	demander	*demaunday*	
to refuse	refuser	*reuhfuzay*	
to believe	croire	*crouahr*	cru
to hear	entendre	*ahn–tahn–dr*	
to forget	oublier	*oobleeay*	
to wish	vouloir	*voolouahr*	
to be able	pouvoir	*poovouahr*	
to desire	désirer	*dayzeeray*	
to command	commander	*kommahngday*	

ENGLISH	FRENCH	PRONUNCIATION	PAST PARTICIPLE OF IRREGULAR VERBS
to obey	obéir	*obayeer*	
to wish	souhaiter	*sooaytay*	
to love	aimer	*aimay*	
to hope	espérer	*espayray*	
to give	donner	*donnay*	
to return	rendre	*raundr*	
to receive	recevoir	*ressevoauhr*	reçu
to thank	remercier	*reumairseeay*	
to beat	battre	*bahtr*	battu
to weep	pleurer	*pleuhray*	
to sigh	soupirer	*soopeeray*	
to regret	regretter	*reuhgrutay*	
to laugh	rire	*reer*	ri
to live	vivre	*veevr*	vécu
to die	mourir	*mouhreer*	mort
to feel	sentir	*saunteer*	
to touch	toucher	*tooshay*	
to see	voir	*vouahr*	vu
to hear	entendre	*auntaundr*	
to meet	rencontrer	*rauncongtray*	
to run	courir	*cooreer*	couru
to jump	sauter	*sotay*	
to fall	tomber	*tombay*	
to lift	lever	*lehvay*	
to dance	danser	*dansay*	
to sleep	dormir	*dormeer*	dormi
to draw	tirer	*teeray*	
to push	pousser	*poohsay*	
to show	montrer	*mongtray*	
to hide	cacher	*cashay*	
to present	présenter	*praysauntay*	

ENGLISH	FRENCH	PRONUNCIATION	PAST PARTICIPLE OF IRREGULAR VERBS
to take	prendre	*praundr*	pris
to accept	accepter	*acceptay*	
to spoil	gâter	*gahtay*	
to throw	jeter	*jeuhtay*	
to lose	perdre	*pairdr*	
to look for	chercher	*shairshay*	
to find	trouver	*troovay*	
to travel	voyager	*voyahjeai*	
to ring	sonner	*sonnay*	
to open	ouvrir	*oovreer*	ouvert
to smoke	fumer	*fumay*	
to buy	acheter	*ashtay*	
to sell	vendre	*vaundr*	
to pay	payer	*payay*	
to lend	prêter	*praytay*	
to borrow	emprunter	*aumpruntay*	
to exchange	changer	*jhaungjai*	
to rob	voler	*volay*	
to read	lire	*leer*	
to calculate	compter	*congtay*	
to write	écrire	*aycreer*	écrit
to sign	signer	*seenay*	
to begin	commencer	*commaunsyay*	
to finish	finir	*feeneer*	
to work	travailler	*trahvahyay*	
to listen	écouter	*ay–coo–tay*	
to look	regarder	*rehgarhrday*	
to cease	cesser	*cessay*	
to charge	charger	*sharjay*	
to point	pointer	*poangtay*	
to choose	choisir	*shoahzeer*	

ENGLISH	FRENCH	PRONUNCIATION	PAST PARTICIPLE OF IRREGULAR VERBS
to burn	brûler	*brulay*	
to cry	crier	*creeay*	
to groan	gémir	*jaymeer*	
to order	ordonner	*ordohnay*	
to call	appeler	*applay*	
to pass	passer	*passay*	
to listen	écouter	*aycootay*	
to interpret	interpréter	*aintairpraytay*	
to abandon	abandonner	*ahbahngdonnay*	
to accompany	accompagner	*ahkongpahneeay*	
to light	allumer	*akllumay*	
to catch	attraper	*ahtrahpay*	
to limp	boiter	*boahtay*	
to break	casser	*kassay*	
to continue	continuer	*congteenuay*	
to debate	débattre	*daybahtr*	
to hurry	se dépêcher	*daypayshay*	
to depose	déposer	*daypohzay*	
to derange	déranger	*dayraunjay*	
to desert	déserter	*dayzayrtay*	
to last	durer	*duray*	
to cut the throat of	égorger	*aigohrjay*	
to kill	tuer	*tuay*	
to employ	employer	*ahnploeeay*	
to inhabit	habiter	*ahbeetay*	
to let	louer	*looay*	
to recompense	récompenser	*raykongpahnsay*	
to settle	régler	*rayglay*	
to take back	remporter	*rahnportay*	
to push	pousser	*poosay*	

ENGLISH	FRENCH	PRONUNCIATION	PAST PARTICIPLE OF IRREGULAR VERBS
to make fire (military)	faire-feu	*fair–feu*	fait–feu
to go back	reculer	*rehkulay*	
to advance	avancer	*ahvangsay*	
to carry	porter	*portay*	
to lean upon	appuyer	*ahpweeyay*	
to stride	enjamber	*ahnjahngbay*	
to operate	opérer	*ohpayray*	
to make an operation	faire une opération	*fair–uhn– ohpayrahseeong*	
to be wounded	être blessé	*aytr blayssay*	
to understand	comprendre	*kongprahngdr*	compris
to translate	traduire	*trahdweer*	traduit
to know or be acquainted with	connaître	*konaytr*	connis
to ascend	monter	*mongtay*	
to descend	descendre	*daysahndr*	
to go away	partir	*pahrteer*	parti
to arrive	arriver	*ahreevay*	
to go out	sortir	*sorteer*	sorti
to come in	rentrer	*rauntray*	
to fall	tomber	*tombay*	
to know (something)	savoir	*sahvoahr*	su
to suffer	souffrir	*sooffreer*	souffert
to retreat	battre en retraite	*bahtr ahng rtrayt*	
to pay attention	faire attention	*fair atahnseeong*	
to line up	s'aligner	*sah-leeneeay*	
to lie down	se coucher	*seh-cooshay*	
to get up	se lever	*sehlevay*	

English	French	Pronunciation	Past Participle of Irregular Verbs
to sit	s'asseoir	*sahssoahr*	
to wash oneself	se laver	*seh lahvay*	
to be sick	être malade	*aytr mahlahd*	
to be well	être en bonne santé	*aytr ahng bohn sahntay*	
to mend	raccommoder	*rahkohmohday*	
to wash	laver	*lahvay*	
to sew	coudre	*koodr*	cousu
to shine	cirer	*seeray*	
to clean	nettoyer	*nay–toah–ee–ay*	
to shave	raser	*rahzay*	
to shave oneself	se raser	*seh rahzay*	
to have the hair cut	se faire couper les cheveux	*seh fair–koopay lay shveuh*	

PRINCIPAL ADVERBS AND PREPOSITIONS

Where
 Où

Where are you?
 Où êtes vous?

Here
 Ici

I am here standing.
 Je suis ici debout.

There
 Là

He is there.
 Il est là.

On
 Sur

On the ground.
 Sur le terrain.

Under
 Sous

Under fire.
 Sous la mitraille.

In front of
 Devant

In front of the Germans.
 Devant les Boches.

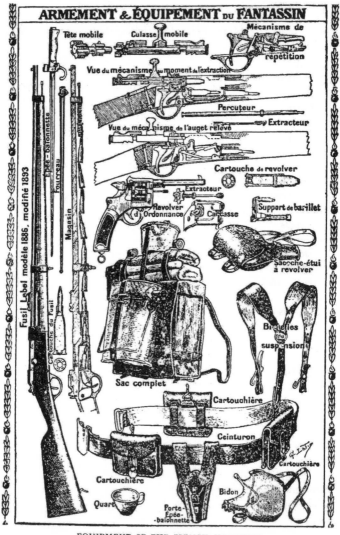

ARMEMENT & ÉQUIPEMENT DU FANTASSIN

Tête mobile — Culasse mobile — Mécanisme de répétition

Vue du mécanisme au moment de l'extraction

Percuteur

Extracteur

Vue du mécanisme de l'auget relevé

Cartouche de revolver

Revolver d'Ordonnance — Extracteur — Carcasse — Support de barillet

Sacoche-étui à revolver

Fusil Lebel modèle 1886, modifié 1893

Epée — baïonnette — Fourreau — Magasin — Cartouche du Fusil

Sac complet

Bretelles de suspension

Cartouchière

Ceinturon

Cartouchière

Quart — Porte-Épée-baïonnette — Bidon

EQUIPMENT OF THE FRENCH INFANTRY

Behind	We are behind.
Derrière	Vous sommes derrière.
Between	A parapet between two trenches.
Entre	Un parapet entre deux tranchées.
In	In the ninth sector.
Dans	Dans le secteur neuf.
With	With the American ambulance.
Avec	Avec l'ambulance Américaine.
Slowly	Distinctly
Lentement	Distinctement
Above	Many
Dessus	Beaucoup de
Below	How much?
Dessous	Combien
Outo of	How many
Hors (de)	Combien de
Outside	Too much
Dehors	Trop
In	Enough
Dans	Assez
Inside	Very
Dedans	Très
Without	Exceedingly
Sans	Fort
Little	As many, as much
Peu	Autant

A little
   Un peu

Much—Beaucoup. To express "very much" just raise the voice. *Never* say "très beaucoup."

More—Plus. Used to form the comparative, as plus grand, more large; tres grand, very large; le plus grand, the most large.

Once, one time
  Une fois

Twice
  Deux fois

Sometimes
  Quelquefois

Often
  Souvent

Always
  Toujours

Rarely
  Rarement

Never—Jamais. Is also used by itself to express "ever."

To-day
  Aujourd'hui

Yesterday
  Hier

Day before yesterday
  Avant–hier

A week ago
  Il y a une semaine

Fifteen days ago
  Il y a quinze jours

To-morrow
  Demain

Day after to-morrow
  Après demain

In a week
  Dans une semaine

In fifteen days
  Dans quinze jours

Now
  Maintenant

In a few minutes
  Dans quelques minutes

Later
  Plus tard

There is *or* there are.
  Il y a

Ago (referring to past time)
  Il y a

THE DAYS OF THE WEEK, LES JOURS DE LA SEMAINE

Monday	Lundi (*lung–dee*)
Tuesday	Mardi (*mahr–dee*)
Wednesday	Mercredi (*marecrr–dee*)
Thursday	Jeudi (*jeuh–dee*)
Friday	Vendredi (*vahngdr–dee*)
Saturday	Samedi (*sam–dee*)
Sunday	Dimanche (*deemansh*)

MONTHS, MOIS

January	Janvier (*jahng–vee–ay*)
February	Février (*fah–vree–ay*)
March	Mars (*marse*)
April	Avril (*ah–vreel*)
May	Mai (*may*)
June	Juin (*jweng*)
July	Juillet (*jwee–yay*)
August	Août (*oo*)
September	Septembre (*septahmbrr*)
October	Octobre (*octobrr*)
November	Novembre (*novahmbrr*)
December	Decembre (*day–sahmbrr*)

SEASONS, SAISONS

C'est le printemps	It is spring
C'était l'hiver	It was winter
Ce sera l'été	It will be summer
Et ensuite l'automne	And next the autumn

MEASURES AND WEIGHTS

3 feet, 3.37 inches	1 mètre
0.03947 inch	1 millimètre
1094 yards	1 kilomètre
1.0567 quarts	1 litre
half of the litre	demi litre
2.204 lbs. avoirdupois	1 kilogramme
half of the kilogramme	demi kilogramme
15.4325 grains troy	1 gramme

CARDINAL POINTS

North	Nord
South	Sud
East	Est
West	Ouest

FRENCH AND BELGIUM MONEY

1 penny	5 centimes (copper)
2 pennies	10 centimes (copper)
1 nickel	25 centimes (nickel)
1 dime	50 centimes (silver)
20 cents	1 franc (silver or paper)
40 cents	2 francs (silver or paper)
1 dollar	5 francs (silver or paper)
2 dollars	10 francs (gold or paper)
4 dollars	20 francs (gold or paper)
20 dollars	100 francs (paper)
100 dollars	500 francs (paper)

Anything above this denomination is of no interest
to soldiers; especially during war.

The easiest way to calculate is to multiply your dollars by five to obtain francs, or to divide your francs by five in order to ascertain the amount in United States money, except exchange which is in favor of the latter and varies according to market quotations.

II

Phrases For Many Occasions

The following conversations or dialogues are given to acquaint the student with a practical vocabulary that will enable him to carry on and understand a daily conversation, and with which he can procure for himself most of his daily needs.

It will familiarize him with the various forms of greeting, of politeness, and of the niceties and mannerisms, of which he would have an immediate demand, should he ever be among a French speaking people. These things are essential if he expects to be shown cordiality while on the continent. Do not be stingy in the use of such expressions as "Oui Monsieur," "Non Monsieur," "Pardon Monsieur," or the like, as they will save much trouble and many dollars.

The conversations will be such as would have to be used should a person journey from this country to the trenches in France. The translations will be literal to a large extent.

FORMS OF POLITENESS

Good morning, good day, good afternoon.
    Bonjour (*bong–joor*).

Good evening.
    Bonsoir (*bong–sooahr*).

Good night (just before retiring).
    Bonne nuit (*bonwee*).

Good-bye.
    Au revoir (*ore–voahr*).

Farewell.
  Adieu (*ah–dee–euh*).
How are you?
  Comment vous portez–vous? (*kommaung voo portay–voo*).
Very well.
  Très bien (*tray bee–ang*).
Thank you.
  Merci (*mair–see*).
And you?
  Et vous? (*ay voo*).
Quite well.
  Assez bien (*assay–bee–ang*).
I thank you.
  Je vous remercie (*jeh voo–reh–mair–see*).
If you please.
  S'il vous plaît (*seel–voo play*).
Yes, sir.
  Oui, monsieur (*wee meh–see–euh*).
Yes, madame.
  Oui, madame (*wee–mah–damm*).
Yes, Miss.
  Oui, mademoiselle (*wee mahd–mouah–zell*).
No, sir.
  Non, monsieur.
No, madame.
  Non, madame.
No, Miss.
  Non, mademoiselle.
Come to see me.
  Venez me voir (*veh–nay meh vo–ahrr*).
Come to see him.
  Venez le voir (*veh–nay leh vo–ahrr*).

Come to see her.
> Venez la voir (*veh–nay lah vo–ahrr*).

Come to see us.
> Venez nous voir (*veh–nay noo vo–ahrr*).

Come to see them.
> Venez les voir (*veh–nay lay vo–ahrr*).

Call again soon.
> Revenez bientôt.

With pleasure.
> Avec plaisir.

INTRODUCTION

Allow me to introduce you to my friend, Mr. Smith, from Chicago.
> Permettez-moi de vous présenter mon ami Mr. Smith de Chicago (*Pair–may–lay mouah deh voo pray–zahn–tay monah–mee——*).

I am delighted to make your acquaintance.
> Je suis charmé de faire votre connaissance (*jeh swee sharmay deh fair vohtr ko–nay–sans*).

EXPRESSIONS MOST USED

What is your name? (Expressed in French: How do you call yourself?)
> Comment vous appelez–vous? (*kommaung voo–zah–pehlay–voo*).

My name is—— (Expressed in French: I myself call——).
> Je m'appelle—— (*jeh mappell——*).

Where do you come from? (Expressed in French: From where come you?)
> D'où venez–vous? (*doo vehnay voo*).

I come from the United States.
> Je viens des Etats Unis (*jeh vee–ang day–zay–tah–zu–nee*).

NOTE—In pronouncing "from the United States," count evenly in your mind: day (1) –zay (2) –tah (3) –zu (4) –nee (5).

Where are you going?
  Où allez-vous? (*oo allay voo*).

I know nothing about it.
  Je n'en sais rien (*jeh nahng say reeang*).

Where is your camp?
  Où est votre camp? (*oo ay vohtr kahng*).

What do you say? (Expressed in French: What say you?)
  Que dites-vous? (*keh deet voo*).

What did you say? (Expressed in French: What have you said?)
  Qu'avez-vous dit? (*kahvay voo dee*).

What do you do? (Expressed in French: What do you?)
  Que faites-vous? (*keh fait voo*).

What did you do? (Expressed in French: What have you done?)
  Qu'avez-vous fait?

What is that? (Point with the finger when you say it.)
  Qu'est-ce que c'est? (*keess-keh-say*).

It is. This is.
  C'est (*say*).

This is not. It is not.
  Ce n'est pas (*seh nay pah*).

Like that! (This expression will help you to make yourself understood when your vocabulary is exhausted.)
  Comme ça.

With that? With this? (Used in stores, meaning: What else?)
  Avec ça? (*aveck sah*).

I will see you this evening.
  Je vous verrai ce soir (*jeh voo vayr ray seh soahr*).

Maybe. Perhaps.
  Peut-être (*peuh-taytrrh*).

Until to-morrow.
  A demain (*ah dehmaing*).

Until this evening.
  A ce soir (*ah seh soahr*).

AT THE OFFICE OF THE TRANS-ATLANTIC COMPANY
AU BUREAU DE LA COMPAGNIE TRANSATLANTIQUE

Good morning, monsieur. When departs the next boat for France?
  Bonjour, monsieur. Quand part le prochain bateau pour la
  France?

Wednesday next.
  Mercredi prochain.

At what hour?
  A quelle heure?

At eight o'clock of the morning, precise.
  A huit heures du matin précises.

What is the name of the boat?
  Quel est le nom du bateau?

Is it rapid?
  Est–il rapide?

Oh, so-so! It takes nine days to make the crossing.
  Comme ça! Il met environ neuf jours pour faire la traversée.

What is the price of a passage?
  Quel est le prix du passage?

First class cabin outside, eighty dollars; cabin inside, from sixty to
seventy dollars.

  Première classe: cabines extérieures, quatre cents francs; cabines
  intérieures, de trois cents à trois cents cinquante.

Show me the diagram, if you please.
  Montrez–moi le plan, s'il vous plaît.

Here it is.
  Le voici.

I will take cabin one hundred fourteen.
>Je prendrai la cabine cent quatorze.

It is all right, sir.
>C'est bien, monsieur.

What is your name?
>Quel est votre nom?

Your first name?
>Votre prénom?

Your age?
>Votre âge?

Twenty-five years.
>Vingt-cinq ans.

Your nationality?
>Votre nationalité?

American.
>Américain.

Have you a passport?
>Avez-vous un passeport?

No, sir.
>Non, monsieur.

It is necessary for you of them to procure one.
>Il faut vous en procurer un.

Pardon me. I go to France to join the American Ambulance.
>Pardon! Je vais en France pour joindre l'ambulance Américaine.

Then it is well. Here is your ticket.
>Alors, c'est bien. Voici votre billet.

Have you some baggage?
>Avez-vous des bagages?

Yes, sir, I have a trunk and a valise.
>. Oui, monsieur, j'ai une malle et une valise.

Here are two labels. One for the cabin baggage and one for the hold.
>Voilà deux étiquettes, une pour les bagages de cabine et l'autre pour la cale.

Thank you, sir.
Merci, monsieur.

To the Transfer Man
Au Commissionnaire

Take this baggage to the wharf of the French Company.
Conduisez ces bagages au quai de la Compagnie Française.

All right, sir.
Bien, monsieur.

How much?
Combien?

Three francs.
Trois francs.

It is too much. I will give you two francs.
C'est trop cher! Je vous donnerai deux francs.

All right, give them to me.
Bien, donnez–les–moi.

On the Wharf
Sur le Quai

Pardon, sir, where do they weigh the baggage?
Pardon, monsieur, où pèse–t–on les bagages?

On the right, sir,
Là, à droite, monsieur.

Thanks.
Merci.

Pardon, sir, will you check this trunk for Paris, if you please?
Pardon, monsieur, voulez–vous enrégistrer cette malle pour Paris
s'il vous plaît?

In a moment, sir,
Dans un moment, monsieur.

Aboard
A Bord

Waiter, where is the cabin one hundred fourteen?
Garçon, où est la cabine cent quatorze?

Follow me, sir.
Suivez–moi, monsieur.

Waiter, where is the dining-room?
Garçon, où est la salle à manger?

Waiter, where is the smoking-room?
Garçon, où est le fumoir?

Waiter, where is the drawing-room?
Garçon, où est le salon?

Waiter, where is the library?
Garçon, où est la bibliothèque?

Waiter, where is the office of the doctor?
Garçon, où est le bureau du Docteur?

Waiter, where is the office of the purser?
Garçon, où est le bureau du commissaire?

Pardon, Monsieur the Purser, I desire to place these valuables and jewels in your safe.
Pardon, Monsieur le Commissaire, je désire déposer ces valeurs et ces bijoux dans votre coffre-fort.

Place them in this envelope and sign.
Mettez–les dans cette enveloppe et signez.

Ask them of me before entering the port in France.
Demandez–les–moi avant l'entrée du port en France.

At the Custom House
A la Douane

Note: If you want immediate attention use the following sentences when addressing the custom officer and watch the result:

Pardon, Monsieur the Officer. Would you be willing, I beg of you, to examine my baggages?

Pardon, Monsieur L'Officier. Voudriez–vous je vous prie examiner mes bagages?

Now nine times out of ten his answer will be:

In a minute, sir.
Dans une minute, monsieur.

Where are they?
Où sont–ils?

There they are.
Les voilà.

What have you?
Qu'avez–vous?

One trunk and two valises.
Une malle et deux valises.

Open them.
Ouvrez–les.

Have you anything to declare?
Avez–vous quelque chose à déclarer?

Nothing that I know of. Look.
Rien que je sache. Regardez.

It is all right, close again.
C'est bien, refermez.

LEAVING THE CUSTOM HOUSE FOR THE DEPOT

DE LA DOUANE À LA GARE

Porter, call a taxi.
Facteur, appelez un taxi.

Put my baggage on the taxi.
Mettez mes bagages sur le taxi.

Chauffeur! take me quick to the depot.
>Chauffeur! conduisez-moi vite à la gare.

Hurry up.
>Dépêchez-vous.

I want to catch the express for Paris.
>Je désire attraper l'express de Paris.

Here we are, sir.
>Nous y voici, monsieur.

I am pleased with you, there is a tip for you.
>Je suis content de vous, voici un bon pourboire.

Porter, carry my baggage to the baggage room.
>Facteur, portez mes bagages à la salle des bagages.

This is for you.
>Voilà pour vous.

Thanks, sir.
>Merci, monsieur.

AT THE STATION
A LA GARE

Where is the station?
>Où est la gare?

Where is the ticket window?
>Où est le guichet?

Where is the waiting-room?
>Où est la salle d'attente?

Where is the baggage room?
>Où est la salle des bagages?

Where is the bureau of information?
>Où est le bureau d'informations?

Where is the interpreter?
>Où est l'interprète?

A first class ticket.
>Un billet de première classe.

A second class ticket.
  Un billet de deuxième classe.

A third class ticket.
  Un billet de troisième classe.

One way. Round trip for Paris.
  Simple. Aller et retour pour Paris.

A reduced rate ticket for a soldier.
  Un billet militaire.

Check my baggage for Paris.
  Enrégistrez mes bagages pour Paris.

How much?
  Combien?

When leaves the train for Paris?
  Quand part le train pour Paris?

At what hour?
  A quelle heure?

When do we arrive at——?
  Quand arriverons–nous à———?

When do we start?
  Quand partons–nous?

When do we arrive?
  Quand arriverons–nous?

What is the name of this station?
  Quel est le nom de cette gare?

Do we change? Where?
  Change–t–on? Où?

Where is the lunch-room? (For railroads only.)
  Où est le buffet?

How many minutes of stop?
  Combien de minutes d'arrêt?

On what track is the train for Paris?
  Sur quelle voie est le train de Paris?

Cross the track.
　Traversez la voie.

Look out! All aboard.
　Attention! En voiture.

Let us step in *or* let us go aboard.
　Montons.

This compartment is full.
　Ce compartiment est complet.

Close the door. (Common carrier door only.)
　Fermez la portière.

All aboard!
　En route!

Have you a time-table?
　Avez–vous un indicateur?

Military train. Accommodation train.
　Train militaire. Train omnibus.

Express. Fast Mail. Fast.
　Train express. Train direct. Train rapide.

Coach. Compartment. Sleeping car. Dining car.
　Wagon. Compartiment. Wagon–lit. Wagon–restaurant.

Is this seat occupied?
　Cette place est-elle prise?

No sir, it is vacant.
　Non monsieur, elle est libre.

Well, let us sit here.
　Eh bien, asseyons-nous ici.

A newspaper; if you please?
　Un journal s'il vous plaît.

What is the news today?
　Quelles nouvelles aujourdhu¹?

The Germans sank another American boat.
Les Boches ont coulé un autre bateau Américain.

We will get them soon!
Nous les aurons bientôt!

Paris—Paris—Everybody out!
Paris—Paris—Tout le monde descend!

Say, John, now you must try your French, for I cannot speak a word.
Dites, Jean, vous devez essayer votre français, car je ne peux pas parler un môt.

Call a cab or a taxi and help me out.
Appelez un fiacre ou un taxi et aidez-moi.

To Take a Taxi
Pour Prendre un Taxi

Just utter "Psst" and the chauffeur will drive towards you.

Take me to the Normandy Hotel, Echelle Street, Number Seven.
Conduisez-moi à l'Hôtel de Normandie, rue de l'Echelle, numéro sept.

Porter! Carry this trunk and that valise on the taxi.
Facteur! Portez cette malle et cette valise sur le taxi.

Chauffeur! Go slowly, I desire to see the city.
Chauffeur! Allez lentement, je désire voir la ville.

How much?
Combien?

This is for you. (These are the words used in tipping.)
Voilà pour vous.

NOTE: In France as elsewhere it is useless to bargain with taximen as the clock tells you what to pay. Should you have any controversy just say the word "Police" and the difficulty will be over.

AT THE HOTEL
A L'HÔTEL

Good day, sir.
  Bonjour, monsieur.

Have you a room with bath?
  Avez–vous une chambre avec bain?

On what floor?
  A quel étage?

In front.
  Devant.

On the back.
  Sur le derrière.

Show me the room.
  Montrez-moi la chambre.

How much per day?   Per week?
  Combien par jour?   Par semaine?

With board?   Without board?
  Avec pension?   Sans pension?

Where is the reading room?   The parlor?   The elevator?
  Où est le cabinet de lecture?   Le salon?   L'ascenseur?

Bell-boy! Bring me a pen, some writing-paper, some envelopes and
two postage stamps at twenty-five centimes (five cents).
  Chasseur! Apportez-moi une plume, du papier à lettre, des
enveloppes et deux timbres à vingt–cinq centimes.

Where is the mail-box?
  Où est la boîte aux lettres?

Throw these letters in the box.
  Jetez ces lettres dans la boîte.

Waiter! Bring up some ice water in my room.
  Garçon! Montez de l'eau glacée dans ma chambre.

Wake me up at seven o'clock, without fail.
  Réveillez-moi à sept heures, sans faute.

My bill, if you please.
  Ma note, s'il vous plaît.

Forward my mail to——.
  Faites suivre mon courrier à——.

Good-bye!
  Au Revoir!

FURNISHED ROOM FOR RENT
CHAMBRE GARNIE A LOUER

Good-day sir—madam. (Never forget to salute wherever you go.)
  Bonjour monsieur—madame.

Have you a furnished room for rent?
  Avez-vous une chambre garnie à louer?

On what floor?
  A quel étage?

It is too high.
  C'est trop haut.

Show it to me.
  Montrez-la-moi.

How much per week? Per month?
  Combien par semaine? Par mois?

It is more than I want to pay.
  C'est plus que je veux payer.

I will take it.
  Je la prendrai.

There is a month's rent in advance. Give me a receipt.
  Voici un mois de loyer d'avance. Faites-moi un reçu.

I will come to-morrow.
  Je viendrai demain.

Porter, do you know of a good boarding-house not too far distant?
  Concierge, connaissez-vous une bonne pension, pas trop loin?

Yes sir. Follow this street straight on, turn to the right and the
second house is a boarding-house.

Oui, monsieur. Suivez cette rue tout droit, tournez à droite et la
deuxième maison est une pension.

Thank you very much.

Je vous remercie.

At the Boarding-House
A la Pension

Good afternoon, madam.

Bonjour, madame.

Do you take foreign boarders?

Prenez-vous des pensionnaires étrangers?

Yes sir. How many are you?

Oui, monsieur. Combien êtes-vous?

Three. My wife, my daughter and myself.

Trois. Ma femme, ma fille et moi.

How much do you charge per week, without room, for breakfast,
lunch and dinner?

Combien demandez-vous par semaine, sans chambre, pour le
déjeuner, le déjeuner à la fourchette et le souper?

That is all right. We will commence this evening, and I will pay you a
week in advance.

C'est très bien. Nous commencerons ce soir and je vous payerai
une semaine d'avance.

What is the name of this street? Of this quarter?

Quel est le nom de cette rue? Quel est le nom du quartier?

Where is the subway?

Où est le métro?

Where is the American Express?

Où est l'express américain?

Where is the bank, Monroe & Company?

Où est la banque, Monroe et Compagnie?

I do not know, sir.
Je ne sais pas, monsieur.

Where is the main post-office? Is it far?
Où est le bureau central des Postes? Est-ce loin?

Where is the American Consulate?
Où est le Consulat Américain?

Which is the shortest way to go to the Avenue de l'Opera?
Quel est le plus court chemin pour aller à l'avenue de l'Opéra?

AT THE RESTAURANT
AU RESTAURANT

The best way to enjoy a visit to Paris is to take the meals wherever you are. You can readily see the class of restaurant by the display on the sidewalk which is called in French "Terrasse." The best way to enjoy a meal in Parisian style is to take it on the "Terrasse." Instead of music you enjoy the sight of the passers-by. There are two kinds of service: meals à la carte or fixed-price meals. The bill of fare indicates the price and what you get. The most popular restaurants at popular prices are the Bouillon Duval and Restaurants Chartier which can be found not only in Paris but also in the Province.

We assume that you do not know a word of French. Just say boldly:

Apportez-moi (*ahportay-mouah*).
Apportez-nous (*ahportay-noo*).

and point either to the price of the meal or to the contents of the menu which you may guess as the author did in your country!

The following is a list of the Principal Eatables:

Some fish	Du poisson
Some oysters	Des huîtres
A soup	Un potage
A beef-steak with potatoes	Un bifteck aux pommes
A porter-house steak with potatoes	Une entrecôte aux pommes
Roast beef	Du rôti de boeuf

Roast mutton	Du rôti de mouton
Roast pork	Du rôti de porc
Some roast chicken	Du poulet rôti
Some bacon fried with eggs	Du lard frit avec des oeufs
Some fried ham	Du jambon frit
Cutlets of lamb	Des côtelettes d'agneaux
Cutlets of veal	Des côtelettes de veau
Eggs on the plate (fried eggs)	Des oeufs sur le plat
Eggs with the shell (boiled eggs)	Des oeufs à la coque
Soft	Tendres
Hard	Durs
Scrambled eggs	Une omelette
French-fried potatoes	De pommes de terre sautées
Mashed potatoes	Des pommes de terre en purée
Some vegetables	Des légumes
Some bread	Du pain
Some butter	Du beurre
Some cheese	Du fromage
Some salt	Du sel
Some pepper	Du poivre
Some mustard	De la moutarde
Some oil	De l'huile
Some vinegar	Du vinaigre
A pitcher of water	Une carafe d'eau
A bottle of wine, white	Une bouteille de vin blanc
A bottle of wine, red	Une bouteille de vin rouge
A cup of coffee, black	Une tasse de café noir
A cup of coffee with milk	Une tasse de café au lait
A cup of coca	Une tasse de cacao
A cup of chocolate	Une tasse de chocolat
A cup of milk	Une tasse de lait
A cup of green tea	Une tasse de thé vert
A cup of black tea	Une tasse de thé noir
A cup of hot water	Une tasse d'eau chaude

A napkin	Une serviette
A spoon	Une cuillère
A fork	Une fourchette
A knife	Un couteau
A glass	Un verre
A plate	Une assiette

When ready for your bill say this:

Waiter, the addition, if you please.
  Garçon, l'addition, s'il vous plaît.

This is for you (when tipping him).
  Voilà pour vous.

AT THE CAFÉ
AU CAFÉ

Note: In a first-class French café nothing is served but drinks and refreshments.

To obtain what you want say:

Garçon! Apportez–moi—
Garçon! Apportez–nous—

A glass of beer	Un bock
A stein	Un demi
Coffee in a glass	Un café
A cup of coffee	Une tasse

If you want black coffee just say, "Nature," which means plain. Otherwise, "Avec lait," meaning with milk. Cream is seldom, if ever, used in the cafés. Usually boiled milk is the substitute.

As to alcoholic drinks, experience is the best teacher, but remember that soldiers are forbidden to indulge in anything except wine, beer and cider. Infraction of this order is severely dealt with, to both soldiers and café-owners.

At the Perfumer's
A la Parfumerie

We desire	Nous désirons
I desire	Je désire
A cake of toilet soap	Une savonnette
A cake of Castile soap	Un morceau de savon blanc
A tooth-brush	Une brosse à dents
A box of rice powder	Une boîte de poudre de riz
A bottle of dentifrice	Une bouteille d'eau dentifrice
Toilet water	Une bouteille d'eau de toilette
Tooth-paste	De la pâte dentifrice
Old-style razor	Un rasoir ordinaire
A safety razor	Un rasoir de sûreté
A razor strop	Une courroie
A comb	Un peigne
A hair-brush	Une brosse à cheveux
A clothes-brush	Une brosse à habits
A shoe-brush	Une brosse à souliers

To a Policeman
A un Agent de Police

Pardon, sir, what car must I take for the Sorbonne?
   Pardon, monsieur, quel tramway dois-je prendre pour la Sorbonne?

Go down that stairway and take the Metro.
   Descendez cet escalier et prenez le métro.

At the Subway Station
Au Métropolitan

A first class ticket for the Sorbonne.
   Une première pour la Sorbonne.

A second class ticket for the Sorbonne.
   Une deuxième pour la Sorbonne.

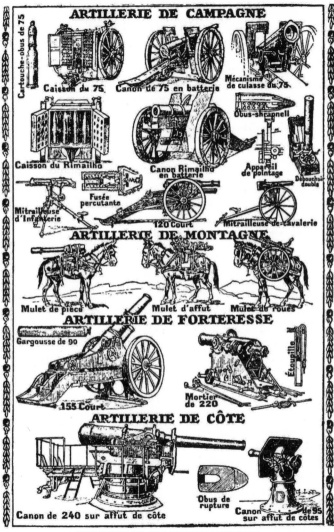

EQUIPMENT OF THE FRENCH ARTILLERY

There it is, sir—fifteen centimes.
   Voilà, monsieur—quinze centimes.

Ask the conductor where you must change.
   Demandez au conducteur où vous devez changer.

Where must I change for the Sorbonne?
   Où dois–je changer pour la Sorbonne?

ON THE ELECTRIC CAR
EN TRAMWAY (ELÉCTRIQUE)

Conductor, a transfer for the Station at Lyon.
   Conducteur, une correspondance pour la gare de Lyon.

Stop me, if you please, at the corner of St. Michael Boulevard.
   Arrêtez-moi, s'il vous plaît, au coin du Boulevard Saint-Michel.

POST AND TELEGRAPH
POSTES ET TÉLÉGRAPHES

Note: The Post and Telegraph service in France is owned and controlled by the Government and the offices are always together.

I want to send a cable to the United States.
   Je désire envoyer un cable aux Etats-Unis.

How much per word?
   Combien coûte le mot?

AT THE POST-OFFICE
A LA POSTE

Have you anything General Delivery for———?
   Avez-vous quelque chose poste restante pour ———?

What is your first name?
   Quel prénom?

Have you an identification card?
   Avez-vous une pièce d'identification?

Yes, sir, here it is.
>   Oui, monsieur, la voici.

Is there a registered letter for ———?
>   Y a-t-il une lettre recommandée pour ———?

There is none.
>   Il n'y en a pas.

Give me three stamps at twenty-five centimes, and two stamped envelopes.
>   Donnez-moi trois timbres à vingt-cinq centimes, et deux enveloppes timbrées?

I wish to register this package.
>   Je désire recommander ce paquet.

Write me a money order for fifty francs for Indianapolis.
>   Faites-moi un mandat de cinquante francs pour Indianapolis.

Cash me this money order, if you please.
>   Payez-moi ce mandat s'il vous plaît.

AT THE BANK
A LA BANQUE

Have you anything addressed to John Smith of Indianapolis?
>   Avez-vous quelque chose à l'adresse de John Smith d'Indianapolis?

I have a letter of credit on your bank.
>   J'ai une lettre de crédit sur votre banque.

Will you cash this check?
>   Voudriez-vous payer ce chèque?

Change me this bank-bill.
>   Changez-moi ce billet de banque.

Change me this American money into French money.
>   Changez-moi cet argent américain en monnaie française.

At the Barber's
Au Coiffeur

Note: Just take a seat and wait until the following sound strikes your ears:

Le suivant. (You're next.)

Then piously take your seat and if you want a shave say:

Rasez-moi, s'il vous plaît (*rahzay—mouah, seel voo play*).

If you wish a haircut say:

Coupez-moi les cheveux (*koopay—mouah lay she—veuh*).

As to style point with your finger and say:

Comme-ça (*kom—sah*).

If you want tonic say:

Friction (*freak—seeong*).

If you want a shampoo say:

Shampoing (*shangpoang*).

As to massage it is the same in both languages. To all other questions say "Non."

To avoid being overcharged give them a bill of five francs and wait for change rather than ask the price. Put two pennies or more, as a tip, in the round metal box which you will see in the shop. The money put in this box constitutes a part of the salary of the French barbers.

Speaking of tips, never forget them and you will be well treated. Do not give much, but always something.

At the Bootblack's
Avec le Cireur

You will never find the shoe-shining stands and parlors in France such as we have in this country. This work is entirely done by boys in the cafés or on the street corners.

If you wish your shoes shined just say:

Cirez-moi (*see—ray mouah*).

Pay from four to six cents according to service.

AT THE HABERDASHER'S
A LA CHEMISERIE

Pronounce boldly "Montrez-moi" (*mon–tray–mouah*) Show me,
and point to the article desired as described below:

A shirt of color	Une chemise de couleur
A white shirt	Une chemise blanche
An undershirt	Une chemisette
Underdrawers	Un caleçon
Socks	Des chaussettes
A nightshirt	Une chemise de nuit
A tie	Une cravatte
Collars	Des cols
Cuffs	Des manchettes
Cuff buttons	Des boutons de manchettes
Collar buttons	Des boutons de cols
Garters	Des jarretières
A fancy vest	Un gilet fantaisie
Suspenders	Des bretelles
A muffler of silk	Un foulard de soie
A wool sweater	Un tricot de laine
A felt hat	Un chapeau de feutre
A straw hat	Un chapeau de paille
A cap	Une casquette
Gloves	Des gants
Some handkerchiefs	Des mouchoirs
An umbrella	Un parapluie
A belt	Une ceinture

After you have made your selection say:
Combien? (*kong–bee–ang*) How much?

Do not forget to bargain with them as this is expected, except in
stores where you read the following sign:

Prix-fixe. (Fixed prices.)

At the Clothing Store
Confections pour Hommes

Bonjour, monsieur! Je désire voir (*jeh day-zeer-vouahr*) I desire to see:

A three-piece gray suit	Un complet gris
A coat	Un paletot
A vest	Un gilet
A fancy vest	Un gilet fantaisie
A pair of pants, trousers	Un pantalon
An overcoat	Un pardessus
A raincoat	Un imperméable
A military cape	Une pélérine

As to bargaining for a price, say "Combien?" (How much?) or "Quel est le prix du cela?" (What is the price of that?)

At the Tailor's
Chez le Tailleur

Do you make repairs?

Faites-vous de réparations? (*fait-voo day ray-pah-rah-see-ong*).

Mend me this.

Raccommodez-moi cela.

I want them to-morrow without fail.

Je le veux pour demain sans faute.

How much?

Combien?

It is too much!

C'est trop cher!

Note: The expressions needed to bargain should be learned without fail as your salvation depends on them.

At the Shoe Store
Au Magasin de Chaussures

Bonjour, monsieur! Montrez-moi (show me):

A pair of lace shoes	Une paire de bottines à lacets
A pair of button shoes	Une paire de bottines à boutons
A pair of low shoes	Une paire de souliers Molière
A pair of spats	Une paire de guètres de cuir
A pair of leggins	Une paire de leggings
A pair of slippers	Une paire de pantoufles
Thick soles	Semelle épaisse
Low heels	Talon bas
Pointed toe	Bout pointu
Half round toe	Demi-rond
Round toe	Rond
Shape wide	Forme large

Give me a pair of shoe-laces.
Donnez-moi une paire de lacets.

These shoes hurt me.
Ces bottines me blessent.

These shoes fit well.
Ces bottines me vont bien.

Can you repair these shoes?
Pouvez-vous réparer ces bottines?

The Time, the Watch and the Clockmaker
L'Heure, la Montre et L'Hologer

What time is it?
Quelle heure est-il?

It is one o'clock.
Il est une heure.

It is a quarter after one.
Il est une heure et quart.

It is half past one.
Il est une heure et demie.

It is fifteen minutes to two.
Il est deux heures moins un quart.

It is noon.
Il est midi.

It is twelve at night.
Il est minuit.

It is quite late.
Il se fait tard.

You are early.
Vous êtes en avance.

He is late.
Il est en retard.

We are on time.
Nous sommes à l'heure.

My watch is fast.
Ma montre avance.

My watch is slow.
Ma montre retarde.

My watch is broken.
Ma montre est cassée.

Give me the address of a good watchmaker.
Donnez-moi l'adresse d'un bon horloger.

Repair this watch.
Arrangez cette montre.

Clean that watch.
Nettoyez-cette montre.

When will it be ready?
Quand sera-t-elle prête?

At the Laundry
A la Blanchisserie

Send my wash to the laundry.
>Envoyez mon linge à la blanchisserie.

What have you?
>Qu'avez-vous?

I have four ordinary shirts of flannel.
>J'ai quatre chemises ordinaires de flanelle.

Twelve collars.
>Douze cols.

Three pairs of cuffs.
>Trois paires de manchettes.

Two undershirts.
>Deux chemisettes.

Two drawers.
>Deux caleçons.

Six pair of socks.
>Six paires de chaussettes.

Twelve handkerchiefs.
>Douze mouchoirs.

Washable white pants.
>Un pantalon de treillis.

Iron well the white shirts and the collars but not the colored ones or the flannel.
>Repassez bien dur les chemises blanches et les cols, mais ne repassez pas celles de couleur ou de flanelle.

Bring back the clothes on Thursday, without fail, for we leave Friday morning.
>Rapportez-moi le linge pour jeudi sans faute, car nous partons vendredi matin.

How much do I owe you?   Take your pay.
>Combien vous dois-je?   Payez-vous.

The Tobacconist
Bureau de Tabac

The tobacco and matches are controlled by the French government and are only sold at certain places by disabled soldiers, retired non-commissioned officers or widows of soldiers who have died in service.

The price of tobacco and the number of tobacconists are regulated by the government in proportion to the population and they are at all times under the surveillance of federal inspectors.

The tobacconist sells tobacco, matches, postage stamps, receipt stamps and paper that bears the government stamp, upon which all binding business transactions must be made. Attention of commissary officers is called to the following fact: Every receipted bill must bear a receipt stamp cancelled by the signature of the seller or the bill is not legally considered as paid. It is a federal offense to accept a receipted bill without the revenue stamp having been properly cancelled.

Do you smoke?
　Fumez-vous?

Yes, sir, I smoke.
　Oui, monsieur, je fume.

What do you smoke?
　Que fumez-vous?

I sometimes smoke a cigar, a cigarette and a pipe.
　Je fume quelquefois le cigar, la cigarette et aussi la pipe.

Give me a cigarette.
　Donnez-moi une cigarette.

I have none.
　Je n'en ai pas.

Good morning, madam.
　Bonjour, madame.

Give me a box of cigarettes.
Donnez-moi une boîte de cigarettes.

What price?
A quel prix?

I don't care.
Cela m'est égal.

I want some good cigarettes.
Je veux de bonnes cigarettes.

Here they are, sir.
Voilà, monsieur.

What else?
Quoi encore?

Two five-cent cigars, a package of smoking-tobacco, six illustrated postal cards, six two-cent stamps and a box of matches.
Deux cigars à vingt-cinq (25) centimes un paquet de tabac à fumer, six cartes postales illustrées, six timbres à dix centimes (10) et une boîte d'allumettes.

Is that all?
Est-ce tout?

Show me a cigarette case and a large pipe.
Montrez-moi un étui à cigarettes, et une grosse pipe.

How much?
Combien?

Eight francs.
Huit francs.

Take your pay from this bill.
Voilà, payez-vous sur ce billet.

Give me back some small change.
Rendez-moi de la petite monnaie.

Let us return to the cantonment.
Rentrons au cantonnement.

PLACES OF AMUSEMENT
PLACES D'AMUSEMENTS

Where is the Grand Opera?
  Où est le Grand Opéra?

Where is the Comic Opera?
  Où est l'Opéra Comique?

Where is the French Comedy?
  Où est la Comédie Française?

Where is the Odeon?
  Où est l'Odéon?

Where is the Theatre Sarah Bernhardt?
  Où est le Théâtre Sarah Bernard?

Where is the concert of the Horloge?
  Où est le concert de l'Horloge?

Where is the Moulin-Rouge?
  Où est le Moulin-Rouge?

Where are the Foolish Shepherdesses?
  Où sont les Folies-Bergères?

We wish to go to the Ambassadors. (Vaudeville.)
  Nous voulons aller aux Ambassadeurs.

What play do they give to-night?
  Quelle pièce joue-t-on ce soir?

Nothing doing.
  Relâche.

Usher (a woman).
  L'ouvreuse.

AT THE THEATRE TICKET WINDOW
AU GUICHET

Show me the diagram.
  Montrez-moi le plan.

An orchestra chair.
Un fauteuil d'orchestre.

A circle seat.
Un fauteuil de pourtour.

A cheaper orchestra seat.
Une stalle d'orchestre.

A cheaper circle seat.
Une stalle de pourtour.

Standing-room ticket.
Un parquet.

A first gallery ticket.
Une première galerie.

A second gallery ticket.
Une deuxième galerie.

A third gallery ticket.
Une troisième galerie.

A paradise ticket.
Un paradis.

A box.
Une loge.

At what time does the play begin?
A quelle heure commence la représentation?

How many acts? Between acts.
Combien d'actes? Entr'actes.

Entrance. Exit.
Entrée. Sortie.

It is customary in France to go out between acts and promenade in the foyer or to go to a café, which usually is at the entrance of a theatre.

III

Phrases for All Branches of the Service

THE ALLIES

The French	Les Français (*lay franbg–say*)
The Belgians	Les Belges (*lay belj*)
The English	Les Anglais (*lay–zahn–glay*)
The Italians	Les Italiens (*lay–zee–tah–lee–ang*)
The Russians	Les Russes (*lay ruhss*)
The Americans	Les Américains (*lay zah–mai–ree–kang*)
The Germans	Les Allemands (*lay–zahl–mahng*)
(Boches)	(Boches) (*bosh*)
The Austrians	Les Autrichiens (*lay–zoh–tree–she–ang*)
The Turks	Les Turcs (*lay Tuhrk*)

RANKS OF THE FRENCH ARMY

Soldier.
Soldat.

Corporal.
Caporal.

Quartermaster Corporal.
Caporal-Fourrier.

Sergeant.
Sergent.

Mail Sergeant.
Sergent-Vaguemestre.

Quartermaster Sergeant.
Sergent-Fourrier.

Sergeant-Major.
Sergent-Major.

Adjutant. (The Adjutant is the highest non-commissioned officer.)
  Adjutant.

Mail Adjutant.
  Adjutant-Vaguemestre.

Second Lieutenant.
  Sous-Lieutenant.

Lieutenant.
  Lieutenant.

Second Captain.
  Capitaine Adjutant Major.

Commanding Captain.
  Capitaine Commandant.

Paymaster Captain.
  Capitaine Trésorier.

Major.
  Commandant.

Major commanding the garrison.
  Commandant d'Armes ou de la Place.

Lieutenant-Colonel.
  Lieutenant-Colonel.

Colonel.
  Colonel.

Brigadier-General.
  Général de Brigade.

Division General.
  Général de Division.

General commanding an Army Corps.
  Général Commandant de Corps d'Armée.

Chief General or Commanding General.
  Généralissime.

Marshal of France.
> Maréchal de France.

Secretary of War.
> Ministre de la Guerre.

President.
> Président de la République.

How to Address Army Men

When addressing a non-commissioned officer always say:

"Yes, Corporal," "Yes, Sergeant," "Yes, Chef" (meaning Sergeant-Major).

And from Adjutant to General say:

"Yes, my Adjutant," "Yes, my Lieutenant," "Yes, my Capitaine," "Yes, my General."

By using the word "Sir" or "Mr." a uniformed man would appear clumsy.

We also have:

Staff Officer.
> Officier d'Etat-Major.

Orderly Officer or Aide-de-camp.
> Officier d'Ordonnance.

Army Vocabulary

aide de camp	aide de camp
arrest (to)	arrêter
under arrest	être arrêté
artillery man	artilleur
aviation	aviation
aviator	avion
band	musique militaire
band master	chef de musique
barrack	la caserne
beating to arms	sonner la générale

Army Vocabulary

beating the assembly	sonner l'assemblée
beating the call	sonner l'appel
beating the dinner	sonner la soupe
beating the fall in	sonner l'assemblée
beating the retreat or tattoo	sonner la retraite
boot and saddle	boute-selle
bugle or	clairon (infantry)
bugler	trompette (cavalry)
call (to)	appeler
roll call	l'appel
canteen	la cantine
canteen keeper	le cantinier
	la cantinière
column	la colonne
command (to)	commander
command (a)	un ordre
commissary	l'intendant militaire
commissary general	l'intendant général
court martial	le conseil de guerre
detachment	détachement
drum	tambour
drum-major	tambour-major
drummer	le tambour
duty	service
on duty	de service
engineer	soldat de génie
engineer officer	officier de génie
engineer regiment	régiment de génie
farrier	maréchal-ferrant
fifer	fifre
file	la or une fil
flank	flanc
furlough	congé

Army Vocabulary

garrison	garnison
guard	la garde
guard (to)	garder
guard-room	le corps de garde
gunner	le canonnier
leave	permission
leave (to)	partir
leave (sick)	congé de convalescence
legion foreign	légion étrangère
line (first)	première ligne
line (second)	deuxième ligne
line (third)	troisième ligne
non-commissioned officer	sous-officier
full pay	solde entière
half pay	demi-solde
officer on duty	officier de service
soldier on duty	soldat de ronde
attacking party	colonne d'attaque
reserve column	colonne de réserve
firing party	feu de peloton
aviation corps	corps d'aviation
flying squad	escadrille d'aviation
patrol	la patrouille
platoon	le peloton
bridge-builder	le pontonier
sector	le secteur
sentinel	la sentinelle
scout	l'éclaireur
sergeant	sergent
instructor	instructeur
sergeant-major	sergent-major
soldier	soldat
squadron	escadron

ARMY VOCABULARY

store-keeper	le garde-magasin
surgeon	chirurgien, médecin-major
doctor's assistant	médecin-aide-major
retreat, tattoo	la retraite
military transportation service	train des équipages militaires
cavalry bugler	un trompette
infantry bugler	un clairon
veterinary surgeon	vétérinaire
to watch, to guard	garder
the watch or guard	la garde
countersign	la consigne
wing	l'aile
right wing	l'aile droite
left wing	l'aile gauche
gun	le fusil
cartridge	la cartouche
cavalry gun	la carabine
revolver	le révolver
gatling gun	la mitrailleuse
hand grenade	la grenade
bomb	la bombe
rocket	la fusée volante
shell	l'obus
shrapnel	shrapnell
canon	le canon
cavalry overcoat	manteau de cavalerie
cavalry coat	dolman de cavalerie
cavalry trousers	la culotte de cavalerie
infantry overcoat	la capote de l'infanterie
infantry coat	la tunique de l'infanterie
infantry trousers	le pantalon de l'infanterie
spur	l'éperon
leather belt	le ceinturon

Army Vocabulary

flannel belt	la ceinture
flag	le drapeau
fort	le fort
fortifications	la place-forte
guard-house	la prison
wire	le fil de fer
barbed wire	le fil de fer barbelé
knapsack	le sac
haversack	la musette
blanket	la couverture
canteen	le bidon
tin cup	le quart
spoon	la cuillère
fork	la fourchette
knife	le couteau
kill	tuer
wound	blesser
a wounded man	un blessé
orderly	l'ordonnance
powder	la poudre
surprise	la surprise
strategy	la stratégie
forage	le fourrage
wagon for carrying forage	la fourragère
horse	le cheval
saddle	la selle
harness	le harnais
bravery	la bravoure
recompense	la récompense
asphyxiating gas	gaz délétère, gas asphyxiant
curtain fire	feu de rideau

sap	sape—means a hole dug in a certain way to communicate with the enemy's first trench. Explosion takes place when ready.
cleaners	nettoyeurs—men who throw grenades and bombs into the enemy's trenches.

ORDERS

To arms!	Aux armes!
Carry arms!	Portez, armes!
Present arms!	Présentez, armes!
Shoulder arms—right!	L'arme sur l'épaule, droite!
Lower arms!	Reposez, armes!
Easy!	Repos!
Keep step!	Marchez au pas!
Change step!	Changez de pas!
Positions 9 ft. apart. A movement of the French infantry.	En tirailleur!
Lie down!	Couchez-vous!
Break ranks!	Rompez les rangs!
Draw swords!	Sabre au clair!
Charge with bayonets!	A la baionnette!
Halt!	Halte!
Attention!	Garde à vous!
Right, dress!	A droite!
Left, dress!	A gauche!
In quick time, load!	Charge à volonté!
Forward, march!	En avant, marche!
Double-quick, march!	Pas gymnastique, marche!
Mark step!	Marquez le pas!
Aim!	En joue!
Fire!	Feu!

DIFFERENT BRANCHES OF SERVICE

I am in a United States Regiment.
> Je suis dans un régiment des Etats Unis.

Which one? Infantry? Cavalry? Engineers? Ambulance?
> Lequel? Infanterie? Cavalerie? Génie? Ambulance?

Aviation? Automobiles? Marine? Foreign Legion?
> Aviation? Section d'automobiles? Marine? Légion étrangère?

QUARTERMASTER SERGEANT HELPING THE CANTONMENT OFFICER

Who are you?
> Qui êtes-vous?

I am Quartermaster Sergeant of Infantry. I am looking for homes to lodge my men.
> Je suis sergent-fourrier d'Infanterie. Je cherche quelques maisons pour loger mes hommes.

Which is the best grocery?
> Quelle est la meilleure épicerie?

Which is the best bakery?
> Quelle est la meilleure boulangerie?

Which is the best meat-market?
> Quelle est la meilleure boucherie?

Who is the best vegetable dealer?
> Quel est le meilleur marchand de légumes?

Where is the market?
> Où est le marché?

Do you know of a good stable?
> Connaissez–vous une bonne écurie?

Do you know of a good garage?
> Connaissez–vous un bon garage?

Take me to Headquarters.
> Conduisez-moi à la Place.

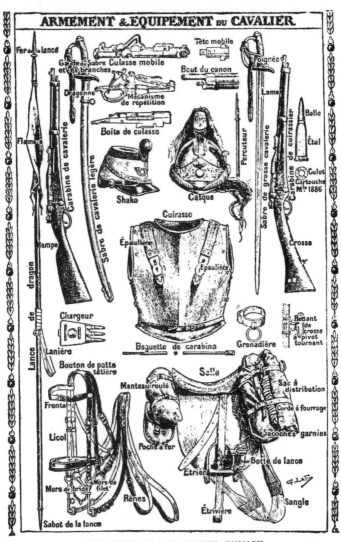

EQUIPMENT OF THE FRENCH CAVALRY

What is the name of the commander of the garrison?
Quel est le nom du major de la garnison?

Where is the city hall?
Où est l'hôtel de ville?

Where is the city hospital?
Où est l'hôtel–Dieu?

Where is the military supply station for forage?
Où est le magasin à fourrage?

What is the name of the mayor?
Quel est le nom du maire?

Where does he live?
Où demeure–t–il?

Which is the best hotel for officers?
Quel est le meilleur hôtel pour les officiers?

My work is done.
Mon travail est fini.

I am awaiting the arrival of my regiment.
J'attends l'arrivée de mon régiment.

My captain, here is my list containing aii information.
Mon capitaine, voilà une liste avec tous les renseignements.

Cantonment officer.
Officier de cantonnement.

I am the cantonment captain.
Je suis le capitaine de cantonnement.

Take me to the commander of the garrison, if you please.
Conduisez–moi au commandant de place, s'il vous plaît.

Follow me, my captain.
Suivez–moi, mon capitaine.

Here we are.
Nous y voici.

Major, I am the cantonment officer of the tenth regiment of Infantry.

Mon commandant, je suis le chef de cantonnement du dixième régiment d'Infanterie.

Here are my papers.
Voici mes papiers.

What are the orders?
Quels sont les ordres?

Sit down.
Asseyez–vous.

How many men have you?
Combien d'hommes avez–vous?

How many officers?
Combien d'officiers?

How many doctors?
Combien de médecins-majors?

How many veterinaries?
Combien de vétérinaires?

How many horses?
Combien de chevaux?

Have you an ambulance?
Avez–vous une ambulance?

How many sick?
Combien de malades?

For this evening your regiment will camp on the drill ground.
Pour ce soir votre régiment campera sur le champ de mars.

Where is your quartermaster?
Où est votre fourrier?

He is down town. He has already hunted for lodging.
Il est en ville, Il a déjà cherché des logements.

Well, go ahead
Eh bien, allez de l'avant.

Leave your papers here.
  Laissez vos papiers ici.

Come back to-morrow at ten o'clock.
  Revenez demain à dix heures.

Good-bye.
  Au revoir.

BICYCLE AND AUTOMOBILE
BICYCLETTE ET AUTOMOBILE

I ride a bicycle.
  Je suis bicycliste.

I drive an automobile in the American Ambulance Corps.
  Je suis automobiliste dans l'Ambulance Américaine.

What is the shortest way to——?
  Quel est le plus court chemin pour aller à——?

What are you doing?
  Que faites–vous?

I am in trouble.
  Je suis en peine.

My back tire is flat.
  Mon caoutchouc de derrière est dégonflé.

Blow up these tires.
  Gonflez ces pneus.

This tire is blown out.
  Ce pneu est crevé.

Where is the repair-shop?
  Où est l'atelier de réparations?

Are you a mechanician?
  Etes–vous mécanicien?

How long will it take to repair this machine?
  Combien de temps faut–il pour réparer cette machine?

The chain is broken.
La chaine est cassée.

Do you have machine parts?
Avez–vous des pièces de rechange?

Front wheel.
Roue d'avant.

Back wheel.
Roue d'arrière.

Tighten this bolt.
Serrez cet écrou.

I want two inner tubes.
Je désire deux chambres à air.

Take the wheel.
Mettez–vous au volant.

A casing.
Une enveloppe extérieure.

Oil your machine well before you leave.
Graissez bien votre machine avant le départ.

Have you an oil can?
Avez–vous une burette?

Have you gasoline?
Avez–vous de l'essence?

Have you water in the radiator?
Avez–vous de l'eau dans le réservoir?

The left cylinder is missing.
Le cylindre gauche ne frappe pas bien.

I do not like this motor.
Je n'aime pas ce moteur.

Clean the spark-plugs.
Nettoyez les bougies.

Transmission-shaft.
Arbre de transmission.

Cog. Gear.
Pignon. Engrenage.

Brake-wheel.
Roue d'engrenage.

Wrench.
Clé anglaise.

Screw. Screw-driver.
Vis. Tourne-vis.

Electric lighting.
Eclairage éléctrique.

Acetylene lighting.
Eclairage acetylène.

Speedometer.
Compteur.

How far is it to——
Quelle distance y a-t-il jusqu'à——?

Show me the route if you please.
Montrez-moi la route s'il vous plaît.

Is the road good?
Le chemin est-il bon?

Our trucks are heavy.
Nos camions sont lourds.

Turn to the right.
Tournez à droite.

Turn to the left.
Tournez à gauche.

Go straight ahead.
Allez tout droit.

I am sick. Find some one to take my place.
Je suis malade. Faites–moi remplacer.

Are you a good chauffeur?
Etes–vous bon chauffeur?

Can you run a truck?
Pouvez–vous conduire un camion?

What horse-power is you truck?
De quelle force est votre camion?

What speed can you get from your motor?
Quelle est la vitesse de votre moteur?

Fill the radiator.
Remplissez le réservoir.

This automobile has four speeds: low, second, high, reverse.
Cette automobile a quatre changements de vitesse: la petite vitesse, la vitesse moyenne, la grande vitesse, la vitesseen arrière.

Electric starter.
La mise en marche éléctrique.

The steering-wheel is broken.
Le volant (le guidon) est cassé.

Is there a garage near here?
Y a–t–il un garage près d'ici?

Do not forget your tools.
N'oubliez pas vos outils.

Above all the jack.
Surtout le cric.

What time do we leave?
A quelle heure partons–nous?

Let us start!
Partons!

Go ahead, jump in!
Allons, en voiture!

Forward, march!
En avant, marche!

I shall have to go by way of——.
Je dois passer par——.

Consult your automobile-map.
Consulter votre carte-automobile.

Slow up!
Ralentissez!

The Touring-Club sign warns us of a hill here.
Le poteau du Touring-Club annonce une descente.

Watch out! There is a turn.
Attention au tournant!

Not so fast!
Pas si vite!

Hurry up!
Activez!

Let us go to one side — draw up to one side.
Mettons nous de côté — garons-nous de côté.

Go as fast as you can.
Allez à toute vitesse.

The radiator is boiling, let us stop.
Le réservoir boût, arrêtons-nous

Madam, loan me a bucket.
Madame, prêtez-moi un seau.

Where is the well?
Où est le puits?

Where is the river?
Où est la rivière?

Where is the spring?
Où est la fontaine?

Look, up there!
Regardez, là haut!

Do you hear?
  Entendez–vous?

It is a Boche aviator.
  C'est un avion Boche.

I have lost my pump.
  J'ai perdu ma pompe.

Solid tire.
  Caoutchouc plein.

Pneumatic tire.
  Caoutchouc pneu

Spring.
  Ressort.

I broke a back spring.
  J'ai cassé un ressort de derrière.

AVIATION

A four cylinder aeroplane.
  Un aéroplane à quatre cylindres.

A monoplane.   A biplane.
  Un monoplan.   Un biplan.

Armoured.
  Blindé.

The propeller is hard to handle.
  L'hélice est dure à manier.

The motor makes a big noise.   Listen.
  Le moteur ronfle fort.   Ecoutez.

Look up there.
  Regardez là haut.

Do you hear, down there?
  Entendez vous, là bas?

What do you see?
    Que voyez–vous?

Look with these glasses.
    Regardez avec ces jumelles.

I shot down a Tauben.
    J'ai abattu un taube.

I came down with a pierced wing.
    Je suis descendu avec une aile percée.

Look at my machine, it is riddled with bullets.
    Regardez ma machine, elle est criblée de balles.

Examine carefully your apparatus, before flying.
    Examinez bien votre appareil, avant de voler.

Are you ready?   Forward.   Let go.
    Etes–vous prêt?   En avant.   Lâchez.

Tighten your belt.
    Bouclez votre ceinture.

Fly high.
    Volez haut.

Can you circle?
    Pouvez-vous cercler?

At what altitude are you?
    A quelle altitude étiez-vous?

What did you see?
    Qu'avez-vous vu?

I saw the enemy.
    J'ai vu l'ennemi.

Where were you?
    Où étiez-vous?

Above———X.
    Aù dessus de———X.

I dropped bombs on———.
    J'ai laissé tomber des bombes sur———

I met———.
　J'ai rencontré———.

I had a breakdown.
　J'ai eu une panne.

I cannot fly, it is too windy—too cloudy.
　Je ne peux pas voler, il fait trop de vent—trop de brouillard.

Give me a good sharpshooter—a pilot.
　Donnez-moi un bon mitrailleur—un pilote.

Do not forget the oil and gasoline.
　N'oubliez pas l'huile et l'essence.

Is your tank filled with water?
　Votre réservoir est-il plein d'eau?

Captive balloon.　A dirigible.
　Ballon captif.　Ballon dirigeable.

AMBULANCE

The stretcher.　The stretcher-bearer.
　Le brancard.　Le brancardier.

Hey! Stretcher-bearers!
　Holà! Les Brancardiers!

Bring a stretcher.
　Apportez un brancard.

This way.　That way.　Let us hurry!
　Par ici.　Par là.　Dépêchons-nous.

Pick up this wounded one.
　Ramassez ce blessé.

Here is another.
　En voici un autre.

Pick him up gently.　Give him a drink.
　Prenez le doucement.　Donnez-lui à boire.

Place him on the stretcher.
　Mettez le sur le brancard.

Cover him with his coat.
   Couvrez-le avec sa capote.

Put this blanket under his head.
   Mettez cette couverture sous sa tête.

Tie him.
   Attachez-le.

Not like that.
   Pas comme ça.

Lay him on his right side—his left side.
   Couchez-le sur le côté drois—le côté gauche.

Lay him on his back—on his stomach.
   Couchez-le sur le dos—sur le ventre.

Stretch out his body.
   Allongez les membres.

Stretch out with care his right leg.
   Allongez bien la jambe droite.

Place his cap and his haversack at his feet.
   Mettez son képi et son sac à ses pieds.

Pick up his belongings.
   Ramassez ses effets.

Carry him quickly to the first relief post.
   Portez-le vite au premier poste de secours.

Hurry a little. Forward!
   Activez un peu. En avant!

Walk slowly—fast.
   Marchez lentement—vite.

Avoid shaking.
   Evitez les secousses.

Lift up together, and walk step in step.
   Levez ensemble, et marchez au pas.

Follow this trench, one back of the other.
   Suivez cette tranchée, l'un derrière l'autre.

Turn to the right—to the left—this way—look out!
   Tournez à droite—à gauche—par ici—attention!

Stop a second.
   Arrêtez-vous une seconde.

Look carefully ahead.
   Regardez bien devant vous.

That's right, let us go on.
   C'est bien, marchons.

There is another wounded one.
   Voici un autre blessé.

Is he alive?
   Vit-il?

I do not know.   Look.
   Je ne sais pas.   Regardez.

Hey, my friend, are you wounded?
   Holà, mon ami, êtes-vous blessé?

Do you hear me?
   M'entendez-vous?

Yes, I hear you.
   Oui, je vous entends.

What ails you?
   Qu'avez-vous?

I have a bullet in my right side.
   J'ai une balle dans le côte droit.

Sergeant, he's alive.
   Sergent, il vit.

Send for a stretcher.
   Faites apporter un brancard.

This one is still alive but that one is dead.

Celui-ci vit encore mais celui-là est mort.

There is one who is breathing. Hurry this way.

En voilà un qui respire. Vite par ici.

He is not dead.

Il n'est pas mort.

MEDICAL VOCABULARY

ankle	la cheville
appetite	l'appétit
arm	le bras
armpit	le desssous du bras
artery	l'artère
back	le dos
backbone	l'épine dorsale
back side	à côté du dos
beard	la barbe
beardless	imberbe
beauty	la beauté
beauty spot	le grain de beauté
bile	la bile
biliousness	bilieux, bilieuse
birth	la naissance
birthmark	la tache de naissance
birth-rate	le nombre de naissance
bladder	la vessie
blood	le sang
blood vessel	la veine
bone	l'os
bosom	le sein
bowels	les boyaux
brain	le cerveau
breathe	respirer
breath	l'haleine
breathing	la respiration

bridge	le pont
calf	le jarret
cheek	la joue
chest	la poitrine
chin	le menton
constitution	la constitution
digestion	la digestion
dimple	la fossette
drowsiness	la lourdeur
drowsy	lourd
drum of the ear	le tambour de l'oreille
ear	l'oreille
elbow	le coude
entrails	les entrailles
eye	l'oeil
eyeball	la prunelle de l'oeil
eyebrow	le sourcil
eyelash	le cil
eyelid	la paupière
face	le visage
fatness	la grosseur
fat	gros, grosse
feeling	la sensation
feature	le trait
figure	la conformation
finger	le doigt
foot	le pied
hand	la main
hip	la hanche
knee	le genou
leg	la jambre
phalanx	la phalange
shoulder	l'épaule
wrist	le poignet

For Doctors

Do you cough much?
  Toussez-vous beaucoup?

Have you vomited?
  Avez-vous vomi?

Gargle.
  Gargarisez-vous.

Do you sleep well?
  Dormez-vous bien?

You are nervous.
  Vous êtes nerveux.

You have fever.
  Vous avez de la fièvre.

Are you drowsy?
  Avez-vous le vertige?

Do you perspire much?
  Suez-vous beaucoup?

You will recover soon, if you are prudent.
  Vous guérirez bientôt si vous êtes prudent.

Swallow that.
  Avalez cela.

Open the mouth.   Don't be afraid.
  Ouvrez la bouche.   N'ayez pas peur.

Amputation is necessary.
  L'amputation est nécessaire.

Put that patient on a diet.
  Mettez ce malade à la diète.

Bring me this patient.
  Amenez-moi ce malade.

Breathe deep—deeper.
  Respirez fort—plus fort.

The ear-drum is perforated.
Le tambour de l'oreille est perforé.

This man will be deaf—blind.
Cet homme sera sourd—aveugle.

There is nothing to be done.
Il n'y a rien à faire.

Do not eat meat.
Ne mangez pas de viande.

Do not drink alcohol.
Ne buvez pas d'alcool.

BANDAGES

Lint. Tampon. Compress.
Charpie. Tampon. Compresse.

Put him in a splint.
Mettez-le dans une éclisse.

Put him in a plaster cast.
Faites-lui un moule de plâtre.

Carry your arm in a sling.
Portez votre bras en écharpe.

Walk on crutches.
Marchez avec des béquilles

Male nurse. Female nurse.
Infirmier. Infirmière.

Doctor, here are wounded men for you.
Mr. le Major, voici des blessés pour vous.

Undress this man.
Déshabillez cet homme

Wash him.
Lavez-le.

Unroll these bandages. Unroll his bandages.
Déroulez ces bandages. Déroulez ses bandages.

Wash the wound carefully.
  Lavez la plaie doucement.

What do you feel?
  Que sentez-vous?

Move the arm up and down.
  Remuez le bras.

All right.
  C'est bien.

Prepare him for the operation to-morrow.
  Préparez-le pour l'opération demain.

Bring him in at nine o'clock sharp.
  Amenez-le à neuf heures précises.

THE OPERATION

Raise the foot.
  Levez le pied.

This toe must be amputated.
  Cet orteil doit être amputé.

Where are my instruments?
  Où sont mes instruments?

Bring me ether and iodine.
  Apportez-moi de l'éther, de l'iode

Dress that man's wounds.
  Pansez cet homme.

Cut his hair.
  Coupez-lui les cheveux

Shave him.
  Rasez-le.

It is a fracture.
  C'est une fracture.

Nothing is broken.
  Rien n'est casse.

It is a contusion.
  C'est une contusion.

Give him a hypodermic.
  Faites-lui une piqûre.

What ails you?
  Qu'avez–vous?

Are your bowels regular?
  Allez-vous du corps?

It will not be serious.
  Ce ne sera pas grand chose.

He needs rest.
  Il lui faut du repos.

This is a fainting-spell.
  C'est un évanouissement.

He is very weak on account of loss of blood.
  Il est très faible par perte de sang.

All his teeth are broken.
  Toutes les dents son cassées.

Send for the dentist—druggist.
  Appelez le dentiste—le pharmacien.

Where is the drug-store?
  Où est la pharmacie?

Are you the druggist?
  Etes vous le pharmacien?

Here is a prescription.
  Voici une ordonnance.

Fill this prescription immediately.
  Préparez cette ordonnance immédiatement.

When will it be ready?
  Quand sera–t-elle prête?

I am waiting for it.
> Je l'attends.

Give me six wafers of antipyrine.
> Donnez-moi six cachets d' antipyrine.

Give me twelve pills of quinine.
> Donnez-moi douze pilules de quinine.

I want a purgative—an emetic.
> Je désire un purgatif—vomitif.

Take that remedy.
> Prenez ce remède.

Take that dose.
> Prenez cette potion.

A teaspoonful after each meal.
> Une cuillerée après chaque repas.

Twelve drops before each meal.
> Douze gouttes avant les repas.

Put that in a bottle and shake.
> Mettez cela dans une bouteille et agitez.

Follow carefully this prescription.
> Suivez cette ordonnance attentivement.

Label.
> Etiquette.

External use. Internal use. Poison.
> Usage externe. Usage interne. Poison.

Send this specimen to the laboratory.
> Envoyez ce spécimen au laboratoire.

Take this man to the hospital.
> Portez cet homme à l'hôpital.

That is all I can do.
> C'est tout ce que je peux faire.

For Dentists

What is the matter with you?
   Qu'avez-vous?

I have toothache.
   J'ai mal aux dents.

Show me the tooth.
   Montrez-moi la dent.

Which tooth?
   Quelle dent?

This one. That one.
   Celle-ci. Celle-là.

Open the mouth.
   Ouvrez la bouche.

Wider.
   Plus grande.

I am going to extract it.
   Je vais l'extraire.

Do not move.
   Ne bougez pas.

I will not hurt you.
   Je ne vous ferai pas de mal.

Oh! You hurt me.
   Oh! Vous me faîtes mal.

Anesthetize that man.
   Endormez cet homme.

That is all right.
   C'est bien.

Give me my instruments.
   Donnez-moi mes instruments.

Pull that tooth for me.
   Arrachez-moi cette dent.

Fill this tooth.
Plombez cette dent.

Your teeth are soft—hard.
Votre dentition est tendre—dure.

An abscess. A complete set. A false tooth. Neuralgia. A bridge.
Un abcès. Un ratelier. Une fausse dent. Névralgie. Un pont.

Your gums are swollen.
Vos gencives sont enflees.

Wash your mouth. Spit.
Rincez–vous la bouche. Crachez.

CHAPLAINS

I am a Catholic Chaplain.
Je suis l'Aumônier Catholique.

I am a Protestant Chaplain.
Je suis l'Aumônier Protestant.

I am a Rabbi.
Je suis le Rabbin.

Can I be of assistance to you?
Puis–je vous aider en quelque chose?

Shall I write a letter for you?
Voulez–vous que j'écrive une lettre pour vous?

To whom?
A qui?

To your father? To your mother? To your wife?
A votre père? A voter mère? A votre femme?

What is their address?
Quel est leur adresse?

What do you want to say to them?
Que voulez–vous leur dire?

Shall I tell them your exact condition?
Dois–je leur dire votre condition exacte?

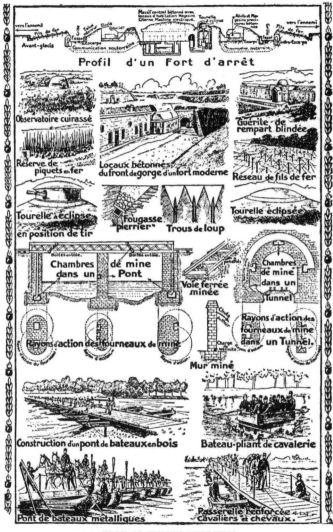

WORK OF FRENCH ENGINEERS

Shall I give them any hope?
  Dois–je leur donner de l'espoir?

Do you wish to see any one else?
  Voulez–vous voir quelque autre personne?

You are in danger.
  Vous êtes en danger de mort.

Have you made your peace with God?
  Avez–vous fait votre acte de contrition?

Confess and God will forgive you.
  Confessez–vous et Dieu vous pardonnera.

Be brave.   Life is eternal.   You have nothing to fear.
  Soyez brave.   La vie est éternelle.   Ne craignez rien.

You give your life for a noble cause.
  Vous sacrifiez votre vie pour une noble cause.

Do not worry.
  Ne vous chagrinez pas.

We will take care of your children and family with the help of God.
  Nous prendrons soin de votre famille et de vos enfants avec
  l'aide de Dieu.

Let us pray.
  Prions.

You have my blessing.   God bless you!
  Recevez ma bénédiction.   Que Dieu vous bénisse!

I will be around. Send for me whenever you want me.
  Je suis toujours dans cette section. Si vous avez besoin de moi,
  faites-moi appeler.

I am a Christian.
  Je suis chrétien.

Do you read the Bible?
  Lisez–vous la Bible?

Do you read the Gospels?
  Lisez–vous l'Evangile?

Do you read the Talmud?
Lisez–vous le Talmud?

Do you read the Koran?
Lisez–vous le Coran?

He is dead.
Il est mort.

The funeral will take place to-morrow at four o'clock.
L'enterrement aura lieu demain à quatre heures.

Is there a Catholic church around here? Where?
Y a–t–il une église catholique aux environs? Où?

At what time do they say Mass?
A quelle heure dit-on la messe?

I want to confess.
Je désire me confesser.

Show me where the Protestant church is.
Indiquez-moi l'église protestante s'il vous plaît.

I must conduct a funeral this afternoon.
Je dois conduire un enterrement cet après-midi.

PRISONERS
PRISONNIERS

Look! What do you see there?
Regardez! Que voyez–vous là?

I see nothing.
Je ne vois rien.

Look again.
Regardez encore.

Something moves there down (down there).
Quelque chose bouge là–bas.

Who lives? Halt there!
Qui vive? Halte là!

Answer or I will fire.
Répondez ou je fais feu.

Throw down your arms.
Jetez les armes.

Throw up your arms.   Approach.
Levez les bras.   Approchez.

Stand there.   Do not have fear.
Restez là.   N'ayez pas peur.

Give me your gun, your saber, your bayonet, your knife.
Donnez–moi votre fusil, votre sabre, votre baïonnette, votre couteau.

Empty your pockets.
Videz vos poches.

Is that all?
Est–ce tout?

I arrest you.   You are a prisoner.
Je vous arrête.   Vous êtes prisonnier.

Forward, march.   March ahead.
En avant, marche.   Marchez devant.

What do you call yourself?
Comment vous appelez–vous?

What is the name of your regiment?
Quel est le nom de votre régiment?

Where is it?
Où est–il?

Are you numbered there?
Etes–vous nombreux là?

Have you a military book?
Avez–vous un livret militaire?

What is the name of your General?
Quel est le nom de votre Général?

Have you many (much) of provisions and munitions in your sector?
Avez-vous beaucoup de provisions et de munitions dans votre secteur?

Tell what you know.
Dites ce que vous savez.

Answer frankly or you will be shot.
Répondez franchement où vous serez fusillé.

Where is the enemy?
Où est l'ennemi?

Show on the map.
Montrez sur la carte.

Are there any troops in the trenches?
Y a-t-il des troupes dans la tranchée?

I do not know.
Je ne sais pas.

Yes, you know, you are lying.
Oui, vous le savez, vous mentez.

If you answer our questions you will save your life.
Si vous répondez à nos questions vous aurez la vie sauve.

Where do you take me?
Où me menez-vous?

To the post.
Au poste.

Why?
Pourquoi?

To question you again (once more).
Pour vous questionner encore.

What have I done?
Qu'ai-je fait?

You will be conducted to the camp, where you will be nourished well.
Vous serez conduit au camp, où on vous nourrira bien

You will eat three times a day. If you will work well, you will be paid.

Vous mangerez trois fois par jour. Si vous travaillez bien vous serez payé.

You can write home.

Vous pouvez écrire chez vous.

Officers

We cannot go into detail as to the commands, for they are almost useless at this time, the troops being constantly in the trenches. We shall only mention those which are used either for inspection or parade or to lead the army to the trenches.

Battalion (company, section) attention!

Bataillon (compagnie, section) garde à vous!

Right dress!

A droite alignement!

Left dress!

A gauche alignement!

Front!

Fixe!

At ease!

Repos!

At four paces, open files, march!

A quatre pas, ouvrez les rangs, marche!

Close files, march!

Serrez les rangs, marche!

For the parade! Company (section, squadron, battery) forward, march!

Pour le défilé! Compagnie (section, escadron, batterie) en avant, marche!

Right turn, march!

Changement de direction à droite. marche!

Column right (left), march!
    Par file à droite (gauche), marche!

By the right (left) flank, march!
    Par le flanc droit (gauche), marche!

Company (section, squadron, battery) halt!
    Compagnie (section, escadron, batterie) halte!

In drilling or marching for parade, the *guide* is generally at the right flank, unless otherwise announced, and the command is:

Guide right, left, or center.
    Guide à droite, gauche, ou au centre.

COLUMN ON ROUTE

On the road whistle signals are generally used; experience will teach them.

Column forward, march!
    Colonne en avant, marche!

Route step, march!
    Pas de route, marche!

Stack arms!
    Formez faisceaux!

When ready to resume the march, the Captain commands:

Assemble, march!
    Rassemblement!

Take arms!
    Rompez faisceaux!

In the open field, the deployment as skirmishers is in constant use. The command is:

As skirmishers, march!
    En tirailleur, marche!

Kneel!
    A genoux!

Lie down!
  A terre!
Rise!
  Debout!
Load!
  Chargez!
Fire!
  Feu!
Fire at will!
  Feu à volonté!
Bayonet charge!
  A la baïonnette!

In the trenches the service is entirely different; the rules and commands are given by the Chef de Secteur (Sector Commander) and transmitted to the men hierarchically.

Artillery officers will have very little difficulty in understanding French commands, for they are the same in both countries since the adoption of the "seventy-five" in 1902.

CARE OF HORSES

We have thirty horses to feed.
  Nous avons trente chevaux à nourrir.
I must have.
  Il me faut.
We must have.
  Il nous faut.
Some hay.
  Du foin.
Some straw.
  De la paille.
Some oats.
  De l'avoine.

Some barley.
De l'orge.

Some bran.
Du son.

Some sea salt (rock salt).
Du sel de mer.

I have three sick horses; have you a stable?
J'ai trois chevaux malades; avez-vous une écurie?

AT THE BLACKSMITH SHOP
CHEZ LE MARÉCHAL-FERRANT

Shoe this horse, that mule, if you please.
Ferrez ce cheval, ce mulet, s'il vous plaît.

Put three nails to that one.
Mettez trois clous à celui-ci.

Lend me a bucket, if you please.
Prêtez-moi un seau s'il vous plaît.

INFORMATION ABOUT DUTIES AND REGULATIONS OF THE FRENCH ARMY WHILE ON MARCH

A little synopsis of the military duties of the French troops on march is given below to acquaint American officers with our system, which no doubt will be beneficial to them while on the Continent.

ARTICLE I. PREPARATION FOR FOOD AND LODGING WHILE ON THE ROAD

The commander of a unit (one regiment or more) must detail ahead the following officers to insure the proper care of his troops:

(1) An officer ahead of the troops from one to two days, taking care of the installation of the troop and food supply.

(2) A cantonment officer preceding the unit by several hours to insure the installation of the men in that locality.

(3) A commissary officer who with the officer of the cantonment takes charge of the food supply. These officers receive from the commander all the necessary instructions. When the unit is small, non-commissioned officers will discharge these duties.

Article II. Mode of Installation

(1) There are two ways of camping. One by pitching the tent and the other by lodging in private houses, by means of a lodging ticket called "billet de logement."

Article III. Duties of the Cantonment Officer

(1) The first duties are to call on the Commandant d'Armes who is the special superior officer having the entire city under martial law. Nothing can enter or leave his jurisdiction without his sanction.

(2) After having had conference with the Commandant d'Armes, and with his consent, he must go immediately to the mayor, stating the number of his unit, and the latter will direct him where to obtain the best lodging for his unit, food, forage, etc.

(3) The Commissary officer then takes charge of his department and when all is in readiness, he must meet the unit at the entrance to the city. All details are taken care of: the condition of the water, where the best fountains and wells are located, the places to avoid so as to assure the best means of sanitation, etc.

(4) All complaints concerning ill-treatment, lack of courtesy or overcharges must be brought to the attention of the Commandant d'Armes, and all the damages, if any, made by the regiment, must be settled before leaving the city.

Article IV. Police Duty

To avoid misunderstanding and misdemeanor, police patrols of the incoming regiment must be appointed.

Article V.   Arrival of the Troops in the City

(1) When a unit arrives, the officers ahead instruct it where to go and what to do so that they may soon be relieved from their fatigue.

(2) The police station is usually used as an emergency hospital for men who have been temporarily disabled on the road. The doctors on duty decide this.

(3) The totally disabled soldiers will be taken directly to the military hospital.

(4) The same precautions as the above are taken for disabled animals under the guidance of military veterinaries.

Every detail pertaining to the food supply, lodging and sanitation is in the hands of the officers who are at the head of the unit.

Article VI.   Certificate of Good Behavior

(1) An officer remains in the City Hall for three hours after the departure of the troops to receive the complaints of the civilians for damages and to adjust them amicably if possible.

If cases are not settled, special reports are made and left in care of the Commandant d'Armes, who will proceed according to military regulations.

A certificate must be obtained from the Mayor stating that everything is O. K. and according to the present war decree, October 7th, 1909, Article 68. This certificate is indispensable. Deviation from this rule would be in a devastated country. Vandalism or infractions of military laws during war time are more severely punished than at any other time.

CONCLUSION

It is hoped that this guide will accomplish its purpose in that it may acquaint its readers with the expressions of daily conversation, and with the spirit and fervor of the French language itself.   The hardest thing an American will encounter in the French language is the pronunciation of the name of his own country, the United States. Therefore, keep saying aloud until you are satisfied with your own sounds, which should be given in five even counts:

Les Etats–Unis (*Lay–Zay–Tah–Zu–Nee*).

It is very presumptuous to predict changes in the military organizations concerning the communication of the Allied Armies among themselves, but the motto of Napoleon, *viz:* "Every time I learned a new language I acquired a new soul," seems to have come true. Time is not distant when a special department will be established in military circles, for the sole purpose of communicating directly by means of the native language without the assistance of an interpreter. This will be done by selected men, who will not only know the various tongues, but will also know the customs and characteristics of the people themselves, which is very essential for a clear conception of what is to be done or expected to be accomplished. For instance, when approaching a Frenchmen, be cheerful and you will find him responsive. This will be found to be the same with the Italians, while a Belgian may be a little colder and the English still harder to approach. The Russians will be found to be very uncommunicative. However, by knowing the different temperaments the proper results will be obtained. This applies not only to the officers but to the men in the ranks.

NATIONAL TOURING CLUB OF FRANCE

Founded in 1890

(Recognized by National Decree of November 30, 1907.)

M. Raymond Poincaré, President of the French Republic, Honorary President.

M. A. Ballif, Sous-Chef de bureau à la Préfecture de la Seine, Vice-President.

M. Henry Defert, D.D.L., of the Supreme Court, Vice-President.

M. Georges Pierron, Second Vice-President.

M. L. Bonnard, D.D.L., Secretary of Archives.

M. J. Berthelot, Treasurer.

General Headquarters: 65 Avenue de la Grande-Armée, Paris.

WELCOME TO FRANCE

The National Touring Club of France invites all of the officers and soldiers of the United States Army to come and visit them. We are expecting you and are waiting to show you what we have in La Belle France.

Our General Headquarters are located at 65 Avenue de la Grande-Armée, Paris, and our offices and club-rooms are always open to you for any information you may desire while with us or later at home. We will see that you receive the proper comfort in the best hotels at a price arranged by the Association; that every facility shall be given you for seeing the interesting sights at a moderate rate; in a word, that no unfair advantage is taken of you while on our soil.

Formalities of admission will be dispensed with for the United States Army. No initiation fee will be levied, the only cost being $1.25, covering the cost of postage for the silver club badge, the identification card and the Yearly Review issued for members only.

Official application blanks may be obtained by addressing Prof. C. Michelon, Indianapolis, Indiana, official representative of the National Touring Club of France; or, if you prefer, by communicating directly with M. J. Berthelot, Treasurer, 65 Avenue de la Grand—Armée, Paris.

Civilians will also be admitted as members provided they comply with the formalities, which can be learned by addressing the official representative.

We sincerely hope that the officers and soldiers of the United States Army will take advantage of this invitation, as it is of inestimable value at this very time.

INDEX

INDEX